T0358585

Principles of Commodity Economics and Finance

Principles of Commodity Economics and Finance

Daniel P. Ahn

The MIT Press
Cambridge, Massachusetts
London, England

This book was set in Palatino LT Std by Toppan Best-set Premedia Limited.

Library of Congress Cataloging-in-Publication Data

Names: Ahn, Daniel P., author.
Title: Principles of commodity economics and finance / Daniel P. Ahn.
Description: Cambridge : MIT Press, [2018] | Includes bibliographical
    references and index.
Identifiers: LCCN 2017060988 | ISBN 9780262038379 (hardcover : alk. paper)
Subjects: LCSH: Commodity exchanges. | Commodity futures. | Capital
    market--Law and legislation.
Classification: LCC HG6046 .A374 2018 | DDC 332.63/28--dc23 LC record available at
https://lccn.loc.gov/2017060988

Contents

Module IV: Other Topics   147

Preface

This book is the culmination of an intellectual journey that began more than ten years ago, when I first became interested in energy and resource markets as a young graduate student.

Back in the mid-2000s, with the guidance and encouragement of my Ph.D. advisers, I'd written several research papers touching on energy and commodities, such as non-Gaussian fat-tailed distributions in commodity prices or modeling the game-theoretic reasoning behind the strategic stockpiling of petroleum.

Then, in 2006, I joined Lehman Brothers as an energy economist, and I quickly learned just how much there was still left to learn.

Commodities had become one of the hottest asset classes on Wall Street, and in the space of two years, I observed firsthand on my Bloomberg terminal the dizzying rise of oil prices toward a record intraday peak of almost $150 per barrel in July 2008, followed by their equally rapid collapse to below $30 per barrel just six months later.

Everything I'd learned in school—even core assumptions about demand and supply and rational markets—was sorely tested. Yet even as I was in the midst of reappraising everything I thought I knew, I was disappointed at how cavalierly some practitioners approached the subject. Billions of dollars were being poured into investments by individuals with a dangerous lack of understanding of fundamental principles.

Altogether, the searing experience of extreme commodity market volatility amid the global financial crisis convinced me that a rigorous treatment of the economics of commodities was needed—for practitioners, educated observers, policymakers, and academics alike. I took the opportunity to consolidate both my market experience and academic knowledge and began teaching the subject at Columbia University, and later, at Johns Hopkins University.

But while searching for an appropriate textbook, I was surprised to find that many standard treatments of the economics of natural resources remained highly theoretical, usually taking as their point of departure Hotelling's classic (1931) model. In many of these texts, one would be lucky to find even a mention of financial derivatives! Treatments for practitioners, on the other hand, were often narrativistic and nonrigorous. After some years of teaching, I came to the conclusion that a textbook bridging and synthesizing the knowledge base of these two communities—academics and practitioners—would be quite useful.

This book is the result. That is also why I chose to title it *Principles of Commodity Economics and Finance*, not *Principles of Resource Economics*. "Commodity economics" and "resource economics" are conceptually interchangeable, but the term "commodities" has a flavor of financial practice, which I believe distinguishes this book from other treatments.

To repeat the cliché, the great constant about commodity markets is change. Something is always happening, whether it's tumbling prices for solar panels and batteries, economic restructuring in China, hydraulic fracturing driving a U.S. hydrocarbon renaissance, geopolitical disruptions emanating from the Middle East, or accelerating climate change. There is also a fantastic amount of sector-specific jargon, impossible to cover in one book, used by such disparate actors as speculators in hedge funds, traders shipping physical commodities in bulk, contractors building a power plant, or regulators designing a carbon tax regime.

This book aims to remain relevant for students and practitioners alike by covering the economic and financial *principles* that should underlie practice. I hope this book can become a resource as readers confront the world's many challenges in regard to natural resources.

The book itself is organized into four semi-autonomous modules. After an introduction to basic concepts and a review of the various types of commodities—energy, metals, and agricultural products—the first module delves into fundamental demand and supply concepts, and covers both the workhorse models and where they are problematic.

The next module shifts to the mechanics behind commodity financial markets and how they motivate financial activity. The third module follows closely from the second by diving deeper into the concepts underlying investment decisions around both physical and financial portfolio exposure to commodities.

The last module is a catch-all for additional special topics such as geopolitics, financial regulation, and electricity markets.

In terms of prerequisites, familiarity with the basic concepts of macroeconomics, microeconomics, financial markets, and statistics is required. Also, particularly in the first module, familiarity with differential calculus is necessary, and an understanding of the calculus of variations and stochastic calculus is a plus.

This mathematical basis may scare off some readers, but there is no need to be alarmed. I've tried to balance equations with text boxes and graphs to provide concrete verbal and visual explanations of the intuition behind these concepts. Nevertheless, this book's utility waxes for those readers who have mastered the mathematical language underpinning current state-of-the-art theory and practice.

My own intellectual journey is far from over, but the chapters of this book mark various way stations along it and I hope will also serve as a navigational guide for others. If this is your first exposure to commodities, I am delighted and honored to welcome you as a fellow traveler in one of the most exciting and challenging domains of human inquiry.

Acknowledgments

For a book that has gestated for so many years and in many ways mirrors my own intellectual development, I owe an immeasurable intellectual debt to a large number of people.

I first would like to thank my professors and teachers, who have played a formative role in my education, especially my graduate academic advisers, Martin Feldstein, Kenneth Rogoff, John Campbell, and Rustam Ibragimov, and my undergraduate advisers, Avinash Dixit, Dilip Abreu, and Michael Woodford.

Other professors I am grateful to have learned from and to have received input and guidance from include Roland Benabou, Martin Weitzman, Bo Honore, Mark Watson, Xavier Gabaix, James Stock, Bill Hogan, Graham Allison, Gilbert Metcalf, and Kenneth Medlock (whose research and notes I borrowed heavily from in reviewing certain concepts in this book).

I would also like to thank my professional colleagues and mentors, including Ed Morse, Willem Buiter, Peter Orszag, Nathan Sheets, Bob Rubin, Ravi Mattu, Prakash Loungani, Rod Ludema, Keith Maskus, and other professional contacts and friends from whom I have learned much over the years, including Bob McNally, Adam Sieminski, Michael Levi, Amy Myers Jaffee, and Blake Clayton.

I thank the administrators and colleagues at Columbia University's School for International and Public Affairs and Johns Hopkins University's School for Advanced International Studies, including Dan McIntyre, Ellen Morris, Albert Bressand, Debbie Blevis, Gordon Bodnar, Christina Benitez, Jaime Warren, and Eliot Cohen.

I am grateful to the many students and research assistants I've had the pleasure of teaching and working with on this book, including Ignacio Sterns, Andres Arguello, Cullen Kavoussi, Winston Kung, Lela Jgerenaia, Bruce Iwadate, Khaled Al Masri, Zhao Peng, Jason Ho,

Allyson Cutright, Campbell Palfrey, and Matt Bogdonoff. Special thanks go to the students in my courses on energy economics, infrastructure and project finance, energy geopolitics, and the economics of conflict and national security. Teaching really is the best way to master a subject, and I couldn't have done it without the opportunity to teach such incisive minds.

At the MIT Press, Jane Macdonald and Emily Taber have been steadfast and patient sources of guidance toward my first book, despite the need to prod me periodically for updates on the manuscript. I thank Deborah Cantor-Adams and Laura Keeler for their editorial support.

And thanks to Anonymous, for all others I have inadvertently omitted above.

Finally, I thank my family for their support, encouragement, and love throughout the long gestation period. My younger brother Joseph read and edited multiple versions of the manuscript with the critical eye of a fellow economist and practitioner and the loving patience of a family member. My parents sacrificed everything so that I need sacrifice nothing in receiving the best education humanly possible in the world. I dedicate this book to them.

1   Introduction

Definitions

What are commodities? The word stems from the Latin word *commoditās*, which means timeliness or convenience. From the same root come the words "commode" and "commodious." The *Oxford English Dictionary* defines a commodity as "a thing of use or advantage to mankind; especially useful products, material advantages, elements of wealth."

In modern parlance, commodities commonly refer to physical materials that are economically useful and valuable to the global economy. These materials typically are either extracted from the Earth's crust, such as fossil fuels or metallic ores, or harvested from nature, such as grains, animal products, and even sunlight. Hence the term "natural resources" is often used interchangeably with "commodities," though not all commodities are purely natural in origin nor or all of Nature's goods useful resources. One could also consider intangible goods to be commodities, such as bands of the electromagnetic spectrum auctioned for use by the telecommunications industry or cloud computing power.

Indeed, almost any chemical element in the periodic table can theoretically be a potentially useful commodity. But chemical elements rarely remain in their pure form in nature. Instead, they combine into an almost infinite number of permutations called molecules, some of which are also tremendously useful for modern society.

For example, chain enough hydrogen and carbon atoms together and you will get molecules called hydrocarbons. If the chain is long and heavy enough, the hydrocarbons become liquid at room temperature and pressure, yielding the familiar petroleum oil that powers our automobiles, trains, and aircraft.

To give another example, when iron is first mined, it is usually in the form of iron oxide ore, a mixture of both iron and oxygen. This reddish hued stuff is convenient to store and transport before it is finally smelted and mixed with carbon atoms from coke to make the steel that supports our buildings and bridges.

Yet even more complicated organic structures are also widely used commodities. An example is the rice grain, which feeds billions of people around the world. Zooming in on the grain with a microscope will reveal intricate biological structures vastly more complex than metallic ores or hydrocarbons.

Fungibility

In addition to their typically (though not always) physical nature and the significant role they play in the global economy, the final defining characteristic of commodities is their *fungibility*. Fungibility implies that the value of a commodity is derived from its intrinsic characteristics regardless of its origin or creation. As such, a unit of the commodity is interchangeable with another unit from different sources.

An example of fungibility is provided by a barrel of crude oil. Small variations in heaviness and sulfur content aside, oil extracted from sources in the United States is pretty much the same molecular combination of hydrogen and carbon as oil extracted in Kazakhstan, halfway around the globe.

Since the consumer values oil because of its intrinsic chemical composition of hydrogen and carbon (which combusts with oxygen to produce carbon dioxide, water, and energy) and not because it happens to come from a particular place, the oil is said to be fungible.

A consumer with an automobile should be indifferent to whether a barrel of oil from one place is swapped with a barrel of oil from another place. After all, the oil in both barrels is chemically identical and would work equally well in an automobile engine. Hence, barrels of oil from around the world are often priced almost identically.

Contrast this indifference to origin of a barrel of oil with the differential attitude toward a finished automobile. Here the origin, type, and history of the automobile can matter significantly. Prices can differ greatly depending on whether the vehicle is designed or manufactured in Japan, Germany, China, or the United States. Other features, such as the make, model, and year of manufacture, also figure in important ways in how a consumer determines its value. Consumers are willing to pay much higher prices to buy a recent premium automobile from a famous marquee name than a common compact.

Another example of a nonfungible good is this book. Physically, books are just collections of ink-imprinted paper. But the true value of a book lies in its informational content and the meaning to be derived from the special ordering of the inked letters, which justify a higher price for some books than for other, physically and chemically indistinguishable collections of inked paper in a binding.

As a last example of a nonfungible good, consider the market for art. An original Picasso commands immensely higher prices than a copy that is virtually identical in every other way, including the same chemical composition of the canvas and pigments and even the same brushstrokes by a master counterfeiter. The painting is valued not just for its intrinsic physical characteristics but for its history. It is unique and not interchangeable with a physically identical alternative. That makes it nonfungible.

Perfect Substitution and Globalization

Why does fungibility of commodities matter? Because fungibility changes the dynamics of the market in which it operates. Economists would say that a unit of a commodity is a *perfect substitute* for another unit.

This fungibility matters tremendously for the economics and markets for commodities. The owner of an oil field in Texas should care a lot if a new oil field is found halfway around the world in Kazakhstan, since all the consumers of the world are perfectly willing to switch from his Texas oil to Kazakh oil because of oil's fungibility.

Meanwhile, the maker of luxury automobiles in Germany cares less if a new factory for subcompacts opens in India, as German luxury automobiles are not perfect substitutes for Indian subcompacts.

And finally, the owner of an original Picasso shouldn't care much at all if a million copies of the Picasso spit out of a printer somewhere as they aren't substitutes at all.

Hence the study of commodities requires an intellectually distinct approach from other economic goods, not only because of the importance of commodities to the global economy but also because of the specially interconnected nature of their markets. They are the quintessential *global* economic good, arguably affected most by globalization. It is the study of these special dynamics that is the focus of this book.

Types of Commodities

As of this book's writing, there are four main categories of commodities widely traded in global markets:

1. Energy commodities
2. Base metallic commodities
3. Precious metallic commodities
4. Agricultural Commodities

Energy commodities include the hydrocarbon fuels of petroleum, natural gas, and coal, but may also include substances such as hydrogen fuel or uranium fuel for nuclear fission reactors.

The base metals consist of the familiar "basic" metals, such as iron, copper, nickel, aluminum, lead, zinc, and tin.

The precious metals usually includes gold, silver, and platinum, highly prized for their beauty and used in jewelry and decorative artwork, though they can also have some industrial applications.

The agricultural commodities can be divided into grains and soft commodities. In turn, grains can be further subdivided into the grass-based cereals (such as rice, corn, and wheat) and the legumes (such as soybeans and peas). Soft commodities include agricultural products such as sugar, eggs, milk, beef, pork, and orange juice. The latter are labeled "soft" because they are fragile and can easily perish if not appropriately stored.

Is this an exhaustive list of commodities? Absolutely not.

There are many other commodities: water, timber, pearls, silk, leather, diamonds, spices ... the list goes on. Commodities can be almost any fungible element or molecule derived from the periodic table of the chemical elements.

Nevertheless, some commodities are more important on financial markets because of the volumes and values being traded in the global economy, both physically and on financial markets through derivative securities. Figure 1.1 shows the overall market value of some selected commodities in terms of global production and consumption in 2012.

As is evident from figure 1.1, the energy commodities, particularly liquid petroleum oil, dominate in value and importance in providing the raw materials to feed the global economy (though obviously the exact global value of any commodity fluctuates according to its price, which can be very volatile).

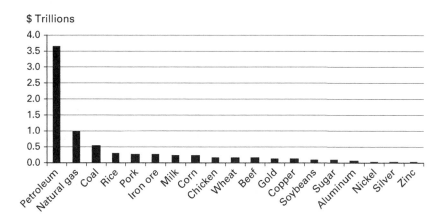

Figure 1.1
Overall market values of selected commodities, 2012.
Sources: Data from United Nations, U.S. Geological Survey, the U.S. Energy Information Administration, and BP.

There is also a highly developed financial market that trades trillions of dollars' worth of financial derivatives linked to the price of oil and other energy commodities. This is primarily why this book concentrates on and draws examples from the energy space.

Meanwhile, many other valuable commodities, such as water, pearls, and so on, have not developed the type of financial depth seen in commodities such as oil.

Other commodities were once extremely important and traded heavily but have become much less noteworthy. Salt, ivory, silk, herring, sperm whale oil, dyes, animal furs, and sugar have faded from their once preeminent positions. The history of civilization is replete with tales of fortunes made and lost and even empires going to war in connection with once valued commodities that subsequently were eclipsed or forgotten as societies and technology moved on. (Box 1.1 discusses a historical case involving sugar.)

Myriad forces cause the various commodities to rise and fall in importance. Technology is an obvious one, sometimes single-handedly creating a societal use for a commodity where there once was none. For example, the invention and popularization of the lithium-ion battery caused usage of the otherwise lightweight but unremarkable metal to surge.

But economic and political factors can matter as well. Cotton has been cultivated since the dawn of civilization, but the invention of the

Box 1.1
When Sugar Was King: Canada, the Caribbean, and the 1763 Treaty of Paris

The Seven Years' War (also known as the French and Indian War in North America) was primarily fought by Great Britain, Prussia, and Britain's allies against France, Spain, Austria, Russia, and allies. The war lasted from 1754 to 1763. The war was described by among others, Winston Churchill, as a "world war" since its combatants, the rival camps led by the European superpowers of France and Great Britain, fought in far-flung geographies across Europe, North America, the Caribbean, West Africa, India, and East Asia.

At its end, the Kingdom of France had suffered military defeat in nearly every theater and faced financial ruin. Yet the British government was also war-weary and wished for peace. In the Treaty of Paris, signed in 1763, France ceded its immense colonies of Canada and its territories east of the Mississippi to Great Britain. In return, France was allowed keep the tiny Caribbean islands of Martinique, Guadeloupe, Saint Lucia, and Marie-Galante.

As surprising as it may seem to modern ears, the French negotiators felt they had received good terms, while in Britain, the statesman William Pitt the Elder criticized the treaty as being too generous to the French, allowing them to maintain their maritime and commercial powers intact.

How could these tiny Caribbean islands be more valuable than all of French Canada?

In a word, the answer was sugar. The Caribbean islands were the world's major producers of sugar. By the late eighteenth century, taste for the tongue-pleasing commodity had swept Europe so thoroughly that a vast industry had emerged extracting the "white gold" from sugarcane plantations, run by thousands of slaves forcibly brought from Africa to labor and die under the hot Caribbean sun. At incalculable human misery, the plantations were incredibly lucrative to their European owners. Successful sugar planters could command immense fortunes and formed an integral part of global trade.

Hence, France readily acceded to giving up all of Canada in return for being allowed to retain some of its prized sugar-producing islands. And when Britain's American colonies revolted against the motherland's rule, France, nursing hopes of revenge against its arch-enemy, allied itself with the rebellious colonists, and the Caribbean once again became a war zone.

Today, with modern industrial technologies, sugar can be mass-produced so cheaply that sugary soft drinks and candies are extremely common and sugar is handed out for free in coffee shops. Many of the famed Caribbean sugar islands, once synonymous with fabulous wealth, no longer even produce sugar and are among the poorest countries in the world.

mechanical cotton gin during the Industrial Revolution allowed cotton-based textiles to become much cheaper, displacing but not entirely eliminating older wool textiles.

The expansion of the Silk Road and Mediterranean trading connections between Venice and the Near East introduced a taste for Middle Eastern coffee into Europe. Coffee was introduced into Brazil only in the early 1700s by European settlers, and now Brazil is the largest producer and exporter of coffee in the world.

It is difficult to predict which commodities will be used in the future or be consigned to the dustbin of history.

No one would deny that water, the essence of biological life, is an essential commodity. Population growth, urbanization, climate change, and other trends are expected to stress the planet's water ecosystems.

However, many governments still maintain municipal water systems that provide water more or less for free to retail consumers. Some experts predict that all water supply will soon have to be traded financially, but the political obstacles to charge for water are immense.

Petroleum oil is perhaps the most heavily traded and valuable commodity at present, but will its position change if electric vehicles challenge the dominance of hydrocarbon fuels in transportation?

Some engineers and architects predict that carbon nanomaterials will become the building material of the future. Will these materials displace the iron and steel used ubiquitously in modern skyscrapers, pushing steel down the same path to obsolescence that other commodities have taken?

These are difficult questions to answer, but at the least, in trying to formulate an educated answer, one would need to know not just the technology but also the economic and political forces driving commodity prices. It is these latter aspects of commodities that this book discusses.

Now let us go through each of the major commodity types currently in use in more detail.

1   Energy Commodities

Energy commodities are unusual in that their value is derived not from the substance itself but from the physical energy inherent in the substance.

What is energy? From the point of view of a physicist, energy is one of the fundamental properties of a physical system, like time, mass, and space. And famously, energy is always conserved in a closed

Box 1.2
Noether's Theorem: The Conservation of Energy and the Invariance of Physical Laws

The conservation laws of physics hold that energy, linear momentum, and angular momentum are conserved in a closed physical system. These laws are quite familiar to any high school physics student. Less well known is the deep mathematical linkage between these conservation laws and the invariance of physical laws to translation.

For example, when we consider the physical laws describing the motion of a bouncing ball, we know the exact same laws should apply no matter where or how we toss it. Hence, all else equal, the ball should move in the same manner if I bounce it in one location or if I bounce it five meters to the left of the original location. Similarly, the laws of physics should be the same if I rotate myself, say, 90 degrees clockwise, or if I wait ten minutes later before I bounce the ball. In other words, the laws of physics are invariant to spatial, rotational, and temporal translations.

Remarkably, the German mathematical physicist Emmy Noether showed that these invariances of the laws of physics to spatial translation, rotation, and time shifts are why linear momentum, angular momentum, and energy, respectively, are conserved. This equivalence is known as Noether's Theorem and is perhaps one of the most beautiful patterns underlying the structure of the universe.

physical system. (See box 1.2 for a discussion of a deep relationship between the conservation of energy and time.)

However, it can be transformed from one state to another. For example, as a ball is tossed into the air at a certain velocity, the kinetic energy of the projectile is transformed into gravitational potential energy before finally being converted back to kinetic energy again (figure 1.2).

Though energy is always conserved, it can come in many different forms: kinetic energy (as mass travels at a certain velocity), gravitational energy (as mass resists the gravitational pull of objects), electromagnetic energy, chemical energy, thermal energy, and so forth.

Hence, from an engineer's perspective, energy is useful because its form can be converted from one type to another and, in the process, energy can do useful *work* (scientifically defined as force times distance). In other words, by harnessing an energy source, we can get things to move in the way that we want.

For example, a counterweight trebuchet converts the stored gravitational energy of the raised counterweight into kinetic energy of the

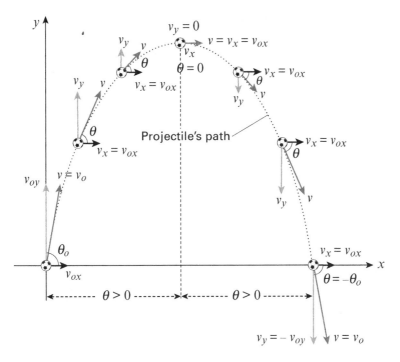

Figure 1.2
The transformation of kinetic energy to potential energy and back to kinetic energy.

fired projectile. An internal combustion engine converts the chemical energy stored in the hydrocarbon molecules inside its gasoline tank into the motion of pistons that propel a vehicle forward.

Indeed, the ability of *Homo sapiens* to harness outside energy sources to do work, move, and shape matter to human will may be a defining characteristic of our species. Other intelligent animals also use tools, have sophisticated methods of communication, and live in large inter-connected societies, but no other animal uses extrinsic sources of energy to the scale and power humans do.

From an economist's perspective, energy is like capital or labor, a fundamental input of the production function. In the classical produc-tion curve framework, economists often lump energy in with capital, but energy is arguably different from other capital inputs such as com-puters, furniture, or automobiles. These items are all highly useful but are not absolutely essential for the basic functioning of society. Our ancestors led long and productive lives without these appliances, but ever since the first humans harnessed fire from wood and other energy resources, the usage of energy sources has been an integral part of our societies.

From the perspective of a historian or an anthropologist, our species has not just relied on its own muscle power but has utilized the energy obtained from burning wood, the labor of domesticated animals, and other sources of energy, including wind and moving water to improve our lives.

But it was not until the Industrial Revolution that humans crossed a remarkable inflection point by tapping vast energy sources in the form of fossil fuels, first coal, followed by oil and natural gas, in service of large-scale industrial production.

Indeed, a bold historian might argue it was the ability of Western European powers—first Great Britain, followed by its continental rivals—to unlock and tap new sources of energy that led directly to the railroads, steamships, and other machinery that underpinned their political, military, and economic dominance over the world for much of the nineteenth and twentieth centuries, a legacy still felt today. Figure 1.3 shows U.S. consumption of energy by source since the seventeenth century.

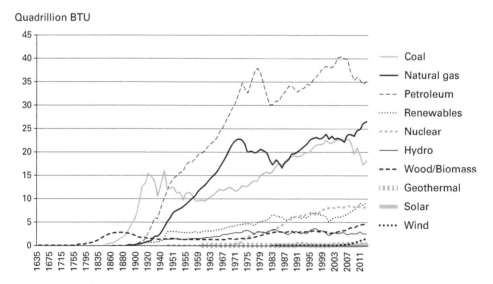

Figure 1.3
U.S. energy consumption by source, 1635–2013.
Source: The U.S. Energy Information Administration.

Remarkably, despite two centuries of technological progress, as of yet no alternative energy source has been identified that combines the cheapness, efficiency, and power of fossil fuels. Despite the rapid rise in renewable energy sources, they still accounted for less than 3% of global energy usage in 2015, compared to the more than 85% accounted for by the fossil fuels. For the moment, we are still living in a hydrocarbon era.

2 Base Metals

We turn next to the metals, sometimes called the "base" metals to contrast with the precious metals (to be discussed below).

In fact, most elements on the period table are chemically metals, but humans primarily use only a handful them. Base metals are sometimes referred to generically as "metals," though they should be distinguished from the precious metals.

Base metals tend to have highly useful physical properties, such as a remarkable combination of strength and malleability. This allows them to be smelted and molded into all kinds of desired shapes and sizes. Their relative sturdiness makes them suitable for use in buildings, bridges, and cars, yet they can be flexible and bend rather than break, allowing, for example, steel buildings to expand in the heat of a hot day without bursting.

Base metals can also be great conductors of electricity because of the free-floating electrons in their atoms. In particular, copper's conductivity, cheapness, and ability to be easily flattened and shaped into long and flexible wires make copper widely used in telecommunications equipment and electric wiring.

Iron is not as useful as copper as a conductor but it is essential as strong material for tools and building materials, especially when mixed with carbon to create that wonderful material, steel. Other base metals such as nickel, tin, and aluminum have various properties of conductivity, strength, and brittleness valued by engineers and builders.

In addition to the desirable properties of base metals when used alone, they can be mixed with other metals to produce alloys that have other desirable properties. For instance, mixing copper and aluminum yields bronze. Mixing copper and zinc produces brass. Mixing tin with a little copper, lead, and antimony yields pewter.

The varying degrees of strength, malleability, durability, conductivity, and hybridizability make the base metals central components of modern life.

3   Precious Metals

Precious metals, such as gold, silver, or platinum, are a special case among the metallic commodities because their value is not necessarily tied to any inherent physical property but to the willingness of others to exchange valuable goods for them. In this sense, precious metals are like gemstones such as diamonds, rubies, sapphires (though precious metals and gemstones can also have industrial applications).

But most buyers of precious metals do not "consume" precious metals in the same way that they utilize other commodities. Unlike gasoline or iron, which is burned up or rusted away as it is used, people buy precious metals simply to own them, such as for aesthetic pleasure mounted into jewelry or stored as ingots. As they are chemically durable, precious metals do not rust away but simply sit there! Indeed, estimates suggest over 95 percent of the gold that has ever been mined is still in circulation.

Not only are they pretty and durable, but precious metals are rare and a conveniently small and portable amount of a precious metal can have a high value. This means they are a practical store of value, with owners confident that the precious metals can be exchanged for other objects in the future. Ultimately, precious metals are valued not for their intrinsic usefulness but because they retain a marketplace exchange value. This is sometimes known as the diamond-water paradox in economics.

In *The Wealth of Nations*, Adam Smith pointed out this difference between "value in use" versus "value in exchange." In his words,

Nothing is more useful than water: but it will purchase scarcely anything; scarcely anything can be had in exchange for it. A diamond, on the contrary, has scarcely any use-value; but a very great quantity of other goods may frequently be had in exchange for it.

The relative scarcity of gemstones and precious metals compared to the abundance of water helps clarify this seeming paradox. Nevertheless, precious metals must be considered a special class of commodities. Rather than fundamental demand-and-supply dynamics, financial and psychological realities such as currency fluctuations, the time value of money, and the dictates of fashion are the most important factors in determining the market for precious metals.

Unfortunately, as fascinating as it is, a full treatise of the myriad of purely financial factors, such as real interest rates and inflationary expectations, as well as market psychology and consumer fashion driving the completely different dynamics of the prices of precious metals requires a whole another book and is beyond our scope. We will largely put the precious metals aside and focus on the more "practical" commodities for the remainder of this book.

4 Agricultural Commodities

Agricultural commodities, the last class of commodities to be considered, fall broadly into two categories: grains and soft commodities.

Grains in turn are divided into cereals and legumes. Cereals, such as wheat, rice, and maize (corn), are the seeds of specialized strains of grass domesticated through millennia of selective genetic breeding. Legumes, such as soybeans or lentils, are the seeds or fruits of nongrass plants similarly grown for human or animal consumption.

Together, the cereal and legume grains form the primary staple diet and source of carbohydrates for the human population. Much as the energy commodities power our tools and vehicles, agricultural commodities power our own bodies.

The soft commodities are an ill-defined category that includes a grab bag of various animal and plant products, among them beef, pork, poultry, eggs, milk, oranges, coffee, apples, and almonds. The soft commodities are distinguished from the other commodities by their "softness," that is, their fragility and perishability, and therefore by the additional cost of transporting and storing them, especially over longer periods of time.

All agricultural commodities, but especially the soft commodities, have the tendency to spoil if not properly stored. The availability of modern refrigeration has lessened this tendency, allowing consumers to enjoy agricultural commodities grown, harvested, and transported from thousands of kilometers away. Nonetheless, it is important to recognize that, unlike a piece of iron ore or a barrel of oil, a bushel of corn or a liter of milk will spoil and lose value if left alone. The biological nature of agricultural commodities also means that their production may be subject to the vagaries of the harvest season, causing cyclical fluctuations in their supply.

Despite the explosive rise of energy commodities since the eighteenth century as the most heavily traded and valuable set of commodities in the world, it was the Agricultural Revolution (which predated the Industrial Revolution by some ten millennia) that was perhaps even more epochal in the history of humankind. Humans' success in domesticating plants, which allowed people to shift from a largely nomadic hunter-gatherer lifestyle in small bands to a sedentary farming lifestyle in larger aggregations, gave rise to civilization itself. The human population on Earth has been expanding exponentially ever since.

And despite horrific episodes of crop failures and famines, global food prices have been on a generally downward trend over the past few centuries. The "green revolution," aided by the use of irrigation, mechanization, fertilizers, and selective crop breeding, has continued the trend. Currently, pressures from climate change, water scarcity, crop diseases, and desertification threaten to break that trend. But human ingenuity has allowed an escape from these "Malthusian" traps.

The so-called "new green revolution," characterized by the use of genetic modification techniques to produce ever tougher strains of crops, shows great promise in keeping food supplies plentiful and affordable for the ever increasing human population on Earth.

Conclusion

This brief tour of commodities has introduced various types of commodities—energy, metals, and agricultural—and their usefulness to the world economy, their inherent physical nature, and their fungibility. Because of their outsized importance to the global economy, the energy commodities, especially petroleum, receive the bulk of the attention for the rest of the book, with a particular focus on their economic and financial dynamics. However, the underlying principles distilled from the economic and financial dynamics of energy commodities are universal enough to be applicable to all commodities.

Module I: Fundamentals of Commodity Economics

In this first module, we dive into the economic fundamentals of commodity demand and supply.

In chapter 2 we cover several standard modeling approaches to the economics of resource supply. Each model addresses different yet crucial aspects of commodity supply, but each model also has its limitations. Understanding all the approaches and their various strengths and weaknesses is important in order to gain a more holistic understanding of commodity supply economics.

In chapter 3 we turn to commodity demand and the factors that affect its behavior across different time horizons. We discuss the various frequencies of short-term cyclical, medium-term secular, and long-term structural factors affecting demand for commodities. We then discuss the relationship between economic development and commodity demand before concluding with a discussion of the long-term price trends and cycles that result from the interaction of supply and demand.

These chapters together should present a complete picture of the proactive and reactive nature of the fundamental forces that shape commodity supply, demand, and their market balancing.

2 Fundamentals of Commodity Economics: Supply

As with other tradable economic goods, there is a market for commodities that brings together supply from producers and demand from consumers. According to standard economic theory, producers attempt to maximize profits by adjusting economic decisions within the production constraints of resource inputs and technological feasibility. Consumers attempt to maximize utility from consumption within the constraints of their budget. The relationship between supply and demand is represented graphically in the price-quantity space by a downward-sloping demand curve between quantity and price and an upward-sloping supply curve between quantity and price. Equilibrium is achieved where the two curves intersect at the market-clearing price and quantity. The price of the commodity is the key economic variable that links supply and demand.

This chapter focuses on the supply side of commodity markets, in particular reviewing the major economic dynamics behind the production and supply of oil, the most heavily traded (and heavily studied) of energy commodities.

We will discuss three major models or frameworks that attempt to reflect observed trends in energy supply. These are Hotelling's model, Hubbert's Peak, and industry supply curves. Although all three have their flaws, each captures important realities of energy supply, which explains their popularity and longevity. But only through understanding all three would a student be able to develop a more holistic picture of energy supply dynamics.

Hotelling's Model: Optimal Production with a Nonrenewable Resource

We begin with the famous model developed in 1931 by the American economist Harold Hotelling (1895–1973), which has become a workhorse of standard textbook treatments of resource economics.[1] In its simplest form, Hotelling considered the economics of a single mine, making significant assumptions on the way. His main theoretical intention was to demonstrate that the equilibrium resulting from a price-taking firm operating the mine under competitive markets achieved a socially optimal outcome. A more detailed mathematical exposition of Hotelling's model and the optimal control theory to solve it is provided in Mathematical Appendix A at the end of this chapter. Here we concentrate on understanding the intuition.

A Simple Two-Period Hotelling Model

Hotelling considered a mine owner who is trying to optimize the supply of resources extracted from a single mine, which is imagined as a single large and known block of mineral or pool of oil. (Some economists have likened it to a simple "cake" to be divided and eaten.)

Hotelling made a number of assumptions to simply his model. These include the following:

1. The amount of commodity in the mine is known and fixed.
2. The commodity is perfectly homogeneous and it takes a constant marginal cost to extract each unit of the commodity.
3. The producer (or mine operator) has perfect levels of control over the rate of extraction.
4. The quantity demanded for the commodity is a simple downward-sloping linear function with respect to price.
5. There is a single and constant interest rate on capital set by markets.

Hotelling's model has been applied to try to explain mine production or even global supply for an exhaustible resource, but the logic and assumptions probably makes more sense for the operator of an amount of stored inventory.

For the sake of simplicity, suppose the mine is a well containing just two gallons of oil. The producer has two days to extract the oil, and it costs \$1 to extract each gallon. He faces a simple linear demand curve, with price $p = 4 - q$ each day.

In other words, if the supply on any day is two gallons, the price will be \$2 (= 4 − 2) per gallon. If the supply is one gallon, the price is

---

1. Harold Hotelling, "The Economics of Exhaustible Resources," *Journal of Political Economy* 39, no. 2 (1931): 137–175.

$3 (= 4 – 3) per gallon, and if there is no supply, the price buyers would be willing to pay is $4 (= 4 – 0) per gallon. Also, let's assume the oil producer faces an interest rate of 10% per day. (This is all highly stylized but it makes the arithmetic easy!)

At its core, Hotelling's model is about intertemporal optimization. The producer has to decide how much to extract each day. Let's call the amount of oil he extracts the first day (today) q_0 and the second day q_1. It would be wasteful to have any oil left at the end of two days, so obviously, $q_0 + q_1 = 2$. What should the producer do?

He could take out all two gallons of the oil today, that is, set $q_0 = 2$, $q_1 = 0$. But that means he will be dumping two gallons of oil onto the market on the first day at the price of only $p_0 = 4 – 2 = \$2$ per gallon, depressing the market price, while leaving nothing for tomorrow, when prices $p_1 = 4 – 0 = \$4$ will be higher because of scarcity. The owner's profit would be the $2 per barrel sale price minus the $1 per barrel cost, or a $1 profit on the two gallons sold today (and none tomorrow), or $2 profit total. Maybe the producer should have waited to produce tomorrow when prices will be higher.

But if he produced nothing today and everything tomorrow, then the same thing will happen. Prices today surge to $4 because of scarcity and depress to $2 tomorrow, leaving the same $2 in total profit. To add insult to injury, the profit would only come on the second day, forcing the producer to wait an extra day to see the $2 profit.

Suppose the owner sets production at one gallon each day. This is more promising. Then prices will be $3 every day, or a $2 profit on each gallon sold, $1 each from the gallon sold today and tomorrow. This means the producer would earn a profit of $2 today and another $2 tomorrow. This is certainly better than the strategy of producing everything on the first day or the second day!

But this still isn't perfect. After all, there is the time value of money. The interest rate is 10% per day. If the miner produces a little bit more on the first day, he may be able to earn a little extra by taking that extra revenue, putting it into a bank, and earning interest over that day rather than waiting to earn that profit tomorrow.

Hotelling's insight is about how to perfectly optimize between these two periods. Economists always consider optimization at the margin. Consider the last marginal drop of oil producible from the well after dividing the remaining two barrels evenly between the two days. Should the owner produce it today or tomorrow?

If he produces it today, he'll get a $2 per gallon profit on that drop today. If he saves it for tomorrow, he'll reap a $2 per gallon profit on that drop tomorrow. But these amounts do not produce the same profit. Because of interest, the $2 profit per barrel tomorrow is closer to $1.82 in profit today once the $2 is discounted by 10%. So it is better to produce that drop today and get $2 in profit today than get $1.82 tomorrow. But the same will be true of the next drop, and the next drop after that, until the producer finds that more production today is depressing prices and his profits today while boosting prices tomorrow.

Hotelling argued that the producer should extract just the right amount of oil each day to make the producer indifferent between today and tomorrow. What is the right price and quantity level that would make the producer indifferent? Well, since time is money, his profit per barrel in nominal terms should also be increasing at the rate of interest.

In other words, the profit per barrel, often denoted as $\lambda = p - c$, should satisfy the following equation: $\lambda_1 = \lambda_0 (1 + 10\%)$. This is the only way the producer is completely indifferent between today and tomorrow and maximizes the present value of his total profits. It turns out that producing $q_0 = 1.1$ and $q_1 = 0.9$ is about the right balance between not overproducing too much in the first day yet biasing toward earlier production because of the time value of money.

The intuition that λ, also known as the *economic rent* or the *shadow price* from the well, must be rising at the rate of interest is famously known as "Hotelling's Rule."

A Multiperiod Example

Let's step up the complexity one notch and consider a multiperiod example of ten years. Suppose that the oil field now has a more realistic 292 million barrels of oil, and that you are able to produce at marginal costs equal to $c = \$10$ per barrel. With an inverse demand equation of $p = 100 - q$, and a discount rate of $r = 10\%$ per annum, what would the optimal production profile be?

Using the same intuition as above, Hotelling's Rule states that economic rent, which is again prices minus costs, should be rising at the rate of interest: $\lambda_t = \lambda_{t-1} (1 + r)$, where $\lambda_t = p_t - c$.

Inserting the prices going backward for every individual period, we use the equation to find the quantity extracted in the earlier periods until we reach the very beginning. (See table 2.1 and figure 2.1 for a better illustration.)

Table 2.1
A Multi-Period Hotelling Example

Time period	Stock (BoP)	Stock (EoP)	Qty extracted (q)	Price (p)	Marginal cost (MC)	Rent ($p - $ MC)	Profit per period (in $Mill.)	PV (profit) (in $Mill.)
1	292	240	52	48	10	38	1,978	1,978
2	240	192	48	52	10	42	2,016	1,833
3	192	148	44	56	10	46	2,024	1,672
4	148	109	39	61	10	51	1,991	1,496
5	109	75	34	66	10	56	1,907	1,302
6	75	46	29	71	10	61	1,754	1,089
7	46	24	22	78	10	68	1,513	854
8	24	8	16	84	10	74	1,162	596
9	8	0	8	92	10	82	669	312
10	0	0	0	100	10	90	0	0
							NPV =	11,133

Note: BoP, beginning of period; EoP, end of period; PV, present value; NPV, net present value.

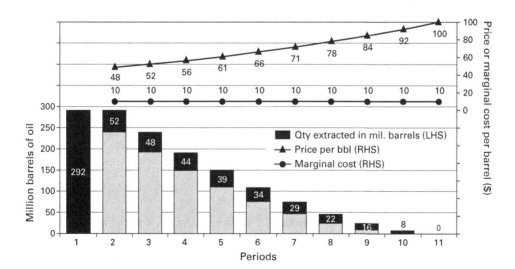

Figure 2.1
Multiperiod Hotelling model simulation.

The value of the resource extracted today must equal the discounted value of the resource extracted in the future, or else there is suboptimal extraction. In other words, the shadow value of the resource must be rising exponentially at the discount rate.

Why should the shadow price be increasing at the rate of interest? The reason to delay extraction of a resource is the presence of a discount rate. As such, an optimizing agent will delay the extraction of a resource only when the appreciation in the value of the capital (in this case the oil itself) compensates for the loss suffered in terms of time lost from not producing today.

A Continuous-Time Approach to Hotelling's Model

Having explored the intuition of Hotelling using discrete-time examples, we now continue our discussion using a continuous-time mathematical model (similar to that used in Hotelling's original paper) to investigate the ways theorists have tried to modify and extend Hotelling's framework. The Mathematical Appendix A provides the full derivation, but to quickly sketch the basic framework, Hotelling considered competitive firms maximizing the discounted value of the stream of profit:

$$\max_{q(t)} \int_0^\infty \left[p(t) \times q(t) - cq(t) \right] e^{-\rho t} dt,$$

where $p(t)$ is the price at time t, $q(t)$ is the quantity extracted at time t, c is the marginal cost of extraction, and ρ is the discount rate.

From the appendix, we have Hotelling's rule in continuous-time form:

$$\lambda(t) = p(t) - c = \lambda(0)e^{\rho t}.$$

The economic rent $\lambda(t)$ from the resource, that is, the price minus the cost, still grows exponentially at the discount rate (See figure 2.2). Note, however, in the competitive market case, the discount rate is the market rate of interest.

It is important to recognize the "fragility" of Hotelling's model. If prices deviate even slightly from Hotelling's rule of exponential growth at the discount rate, then producers should immediately race to produce in order to exploit that deviation and extract the entire mine all at once, since there is no cost of adjustment or storage.

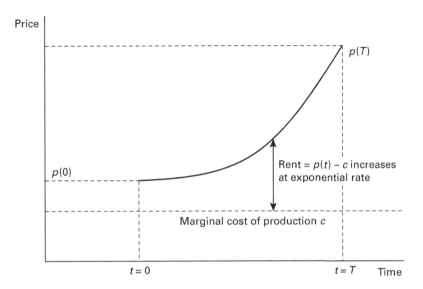

Figure 2.2
Hotelling's rule of exponential growth.

Relaxing Hotelling's Assumptions

Hotelling provides an elegant analytical framework incorporating an important insight into the economics of supply, namely, that of intertemporal optimization. But as we shall see in the next chapter, in practice, many commodity prices seem stationary in the long run; that is, they don't seem to have a clear upward trend. This seemingly conflicts with Hotelling's rule, which predicts exponentially increasing commodity rents (and therefore, after adjusting for costs, prices). In this section we try to relax some of the assumptions in Hotelling's model and see if it helps give more real-world applicability.

Backstop Technology
One simple way to extend the model is to consider possible substitutes for the resource. When the price of extracting a resource becomes equal to or higher than that of a substitute, the substitute is likely to replace that resource in the economy. For example, if the price of fossil fuels becomes too high, people might switch to alternative energy sources as a "backstop," such fusion power or other energy sources. One can also consider backstop technologies as simply a cheaper substitute, such as cheaper natural gas replacing coal. But the important assumption

is that once the switch to a backstop technology is made, there is no going back. The investment into the backstop technology is irreversible (a point we will return to in chapter 6 on real options).

A backstop technology can only be feasibly employed in the extraction process once the price of the resource becomes high enough to justify a transition out of it and into the substitute technology. Accordingly, the payoff function for resource extraction must take into account the cost ($\bar{c}$) associated with the use of a backstop technology, where $\bar{c} > c$ in order for resource extraction to take place using the original technology. As long as the shadow price plus marginal cost is lower than that of the backstop technology, no transition to the backstop technology will take place.

If we consider an exogenous backstop technology b, the instantaneous payoff function would change to:

$$\pi(x(t), u(t)) = \Omega(q(t), b(t)) - cq(t) - \bar{c}b(t),$$

where $\bar{c}$ is the cost of the backstop technology, which is unconstrained in its use:

$$H = \Omega - (\lambda + c) \times q - \bar{c}b.$$

As long as $\lambda + c < \bar{c}$, then the usage of backstop technology $b = 0$. Once $\lambda + c \geq \bar{c}$, however, producers will switch to the backstop technology. There will be an exponential rise in shadow prices until $\lambda(T) = c + \bar{c}$, as shown in figure 2.3. This is a rather boring extension of Hotelling but does remind us that consumers may face substitutes beyond the resource itself.

In practice, however, substitutes are likely going through their own complex supply-and-demand dynamics, and a switch to an alternative (e.g., from gasoline-powered to electric vehicles) is not costless and simple. Furthermore, the development of substitutes is likely itself to depend on the price of the resource, as a higher resource price incentivizes the search for alternatives.

Variable Mine Quality

Owing to numerous geological, geopolitical, and technological conditions, resource mines may not have uniform qualities and extraction costs. For example, onshore oil fields in the Middle East may have extraction costs as low as $10 per barrel, while the oil sands in Canada often break even around $80 to $100 per barrel. How can this reality of variable mine qualities be factored into Hotelling's model?

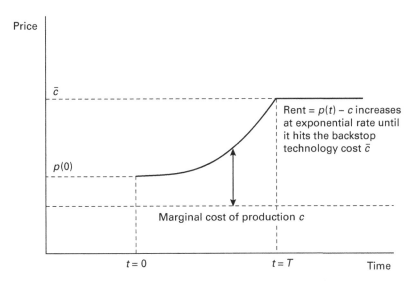

Figure 2.3
Hotelling's rule with a backstop technology.

Consider a firm that owns two mines with different marginal costs of extraction, c_1 and c_2. It can be shown that the firm will choose to not exploit two mines of different qualities simultaneously. Rather, the firm will opt to deplete the cheaper mine first, with the rent increasing exponentially as per the usual rule until it hits the point where the producer finds it more efficient to move on to the other mine. This intermediate time of switching occurs when the economic rent from the first mine exactly equals the rent from the second mine:

$$\lambda_1(T_1) + c_1 = \lambda_2(T_1) + c_2.$$

Figure 2.4 shows how once the switch to the second, more expensive mine is made, the same Hotelling's rule dynamic holds again, now at the higher marginal cost of production.

In practice, there are many reasons why this framework is still too simplistic. Resource producers may face capacity constraints that prevent full and cost-effective extraction from the first mine even if it is cheaper to do so. For example, too rapid extraction from an oil field can damage it by causing its geological pressure to drop too quickly, reducing the amount of oil ultimately recoverable from the field and its long-term value. Hotelling's assumption that firms have fine-tuned control over the extraction rate is an extreme one when producers face numerous short-term geological, technological, and financial constraints.

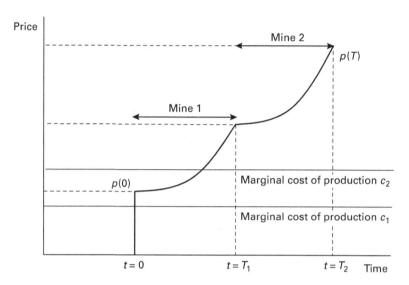

Figure 2.4
Two heterogeneous mines, illustrating dynamic of Hotelling's rule twice.

In the medium and long term, however, firms do have better control over the investment decisions that ultimately determine the rate of extraction. In fact, the recent breakthrough in using horizontal hydraulic fracturing technologies to extract from shale oil basins has given oil companies better control over their production output because the decline rate from fracking wells is much steeper and production is much more closely linked to a firm's drilling decisions.

Market Power

Hotelling's model assumes that markets for the extracted resource are perfectly competitive and that firms maximize their extraction rates as price-takers. In reality, some producers may have the market power to affect prices directly, and Hotelling's model can be modified accordingly. Instead of a price-taking small firm, let's consider a monopolist facing a demand curve. The payoff function becomes:

$$\pi(q) = p(q) \times q - cq.$$

This looks almost identical to the competitive market case, but importantly, the monopolist now considers how his production decisions affect prices in maximizing his profit.

In this case, the first-order condition (FOC) becomes:

$$\lambda + c = \underbrace{\left(p(q) + \frac{dp(q)}{d(q)} \times q \right)}_{monopoly\ price} < \underbrace{p(q)}_{perfect\ competition\ price} .$$

Since the demand function is downward sloping in quantity, the derivative is negative and extraction proceeds at a slower rate than under competitive markets, as the price-setting monopolist adjusts production in order to maximize profits. Box 2.1 goes into more detail on the role of the Organization of Petroleum Exporting Countries or OPEC in monopolistic behavior in the oil market. But we still have from the second condition positing Hotelling's rule of exponentially increasing economic rents.

Box 2.1
Hotelling and OPEC

Why does the world rely on a variety of relatively expensive oil suppliers from different basins rather than on the lowest-cost source of supply? In a competitive market, we would expect consumers to purchase from the lowest cost producer. However, nonrenewable markets do not operate this way. That's because most major oil producers maintain monopolistic control over their oil and natural gas reserves through sovereign state-owned oil companies. Many of these national oil companies (NOCs) are also part of an international cartel, the Organization of Petroleum Exporting Companies or OPEC. These monopolistic producers coordinate their production to affect prices. (We discuss NOCs in more detail in chapter 9.) As a result, the members of this cartel are not price-takers but *price-makers*. The cartel evaluates the global demand curve and the way in which prices adjust to the quantity supplied. By keeping the quantity supplied below the level that would be supplied under perfectly competitive conditions, they artificially increase prices and therefore their ultimate profit. OPEC is a classic example of an oligopoly (though one that faces constant internal political tensions and challenges of enforcement).

Ironically, this allows other competitive firms in non-OPEC areas to produce and sell oil at higher prices than they otherwise would and remain profitable, since they don't have to compete with ultra-cheap OPEC crude. Because OPEC members deliberately hold back quantities of supply, they aren't driven out of the market. Here is yet another example where the elegant theory of Hotelling collides with the messy real world.

We covered various extensions to Hotelling's original framework—
the existence of alternative technological substitutes, the presence of
variable mine qualities and costs, and price-making producers.

Yet two core assumptions remain: (1) that producers have perfect
information about the amount of resource in their mines and the future
trajectory of prices, and (2) that they have perfect control over the exact
speed of extraction. It's as if the mine were not a mine at all but a giant
storage tank ready to release. Naturally, geologists and mining engineers would beg to differ!

It turns out that for most practical contexts, engineering challenges
preventing fine-tuned extraction, a high degree of uncertainty about
the future, and other economic, political, and technological constraints
"swamp" the Hotelling effect of exponentially increasing economic
rents.

Nonetheless, the model does capture an essential reality of natural
resource extraction: that producers will strive to optimize production
intertemporally and that the problem of resource extraction should be
thought of as a *dynamic* problem, not a static one.

Hubbert: The Geologist's Approach

Having completed our introduction to Hotelling's model, we turn next
to the model introduced by Marion King Hubbert (1903–1989). As we
saw above, Hotelling largely ignores the geological and engineering
challenges associated with finding and extracting the resource. Hubbert's approach puts those challenges at the very center of his analysis.
Hubbert, or "King Hubbert," as he was known, was not an economist
but an American geoscientist and engineer. Nevertheless, his model of
a resource basin through a geological life cycle has proven very influ-
ential and surprisingly practical.[2]

Hubbert was inspired by logistical models used to model the eco-
logical dynamics of animal population growth and decay in a Malthusian world of limited food supply. He argued that similar boom-and-bust
life cycles can apply to the supply of resources. (Mathematical Appendix B at the end of this chapter provides the mathematical derivation
of Hubbert's logistical model.) For example, when exploration in a

2. Marion King Hubbert, "Nuclear Energy and the Fossil Fuels," lecture, American
Petroleum Institute, Spring Meeting of the Southern District, San Antonio, Tex., March
8, 1956.

particular geological reserve begins, the rate of growth of cumulative output rises "almost" exponentially as sweet spots are discovered and engineers gain a better understanding of the geology. However, much as the population of animals begins to plateau and then reverses as the food supply runs out, eventually the reserve begins to be exhausted as cumulative production approaches the ultimately recoverable quantity of the resource.

In contrast to Hotelling, Hubbert was not trying to model a single mine. Hubbert acknowledged that each mine may be forced to follow some rigid output schedule according to the stipulations of geology and mine pressure. But Hubbert argued that in a large-enough geological area, a macroscopic pattern can be detected by aggregating the discoveries and exploitation of multiple mines. Logistical growth in production as engineers improved their understanding of the geology through exploration and discovery would eventually hit the limits of the overall amount of recoverable resources in the region.

Figures 2.5 to 2.7 show how the aggregation of multiple smaller mines of various sizes and times of discovery eventually can create an overarching logistical bell curve.

Despite its simple and deterministic approach, Hubbert's assumption turns out to be a fairly good fit for specific geological regions. The Hubbert model for Norway, for example, has thus far been a fairly accurate predictor of the country's lifetime extraction path, insofar as Norway is its own geological region (figure 2.8).

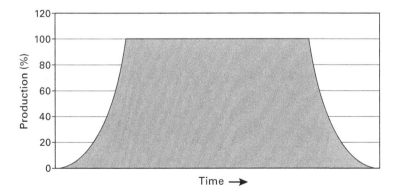

Figure 2.5
Single mine production schedule.

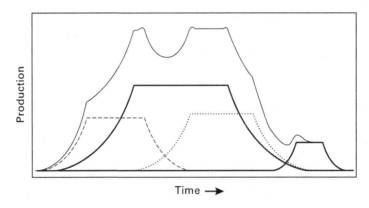

Figure 2.6
Aggregation of multiple mines.

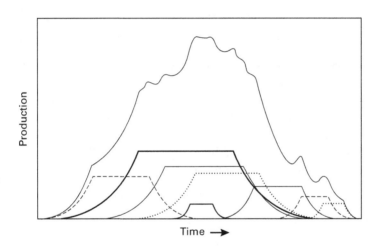

Figure 2.7
Emergence of Hubbert's Logistical Bell Curve.

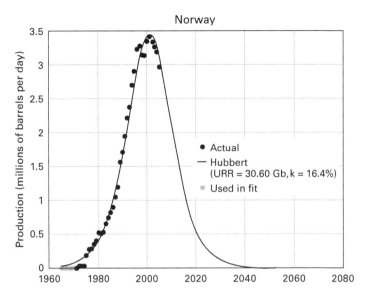

Figure 2.8
Hubbert's bell curve for Norway.

However, when applied to a country like the United States, which is a much larger area with multiple geological regions, Hubbert's model becomes relatively less precise. And most critically, as box 2.2 shows, Hubbert's model contains no mechanism for taking into account advancing technology that may make new resource basins economical, or the fluctuations in prices that may incentivize slower or faster development of the basins in question.

Peak Oil

When extrapolated to the entire world, Hubbert's peak model seems to argue for a definite and predictable point of peak global supply of a nonrenewing resource like oil and eventual Malthusian catastrophe as the resource runs out. Here is where literal applications of Hubbert's model have proved highly problematic.

Perhaps the most egregious mistake is in misunderstanding "technically recoverable" reserves as an exogenous geological estimate of the finite amount of resources left in the Earth's crust. In fact, estimates of the amount of recoverable resources, despite being informed by geological characteristics, are *economic* variables strongly driven by price-based incentives to explore. In other words, as new technology makes

Box 2.2
Hubbert's Curve Broken: The U.S. Tight Oil Revolution

As shown in figure 2.9, U.S. oil production followed the path forecasted by Hubbert's model reasonably closely throughout most of the twentieth century. Indeed, many analysts extrapolated from this extraction history to proclaim that "peak oil" in America was nigh and that production would inexorably decline subsequently. Yet beginning in the early 2010s, U.S. oil production diverged markedly from that predicted by Hubbert's model. This was the result of the unconventional shale or "fracking" revolution, and it reveals much about the shortcomings of Hubbert's model.

Apart from serious doubts as to whether Hubbert's proposed aggregation is applicable beyond a single geological area, Hubbert's aggregation flatly ignores economic forces driven by price dynamics and technological change.

The development of U.S. shale/tight oil was incentivized by higher prices, which spurred technological breakthroughs in combining hydraulic fracturing, horizontal drilling, and computer-aided seismic imaging that made previously known reserves of shale/tight oil economical. It opened up new reserves that were not in Hubbert's initial parameterization, thus "breaking" Hubbert's Peak Curve.

more resources recoverable, the point at which we would say we have reached peak oil gets delayed. Hubbert's model does not consider these endogenous economic considerations at all.

Figure 2.10 shows that in the case of oil, the technically recoverable amount of oil in the world has been steadily increasing despite the constant drain from consumption. Moreover, reserve estimates have increased faster in periods of high oil prices (as companies have become incentivized to search for more resources) and stagnate when oil prices are low.

The concept of peak resource, by ignoring these economic dynamics, stands on shaky theoretical ground. Despite the appealing simplicity of a theory of peak resource that promises Malthusian catastrophe, economic forces and technological progress have trumped any exogenous constraints imposed by nature. It is worth quoting from Morris Adelman, a distinguished professor of energy economics at MIT, in full:

The assumption of an initial fixed stock is superfluous and wrong. Only a fraction of the mineral in the earth's crust, or in any given field, will ever be used. … What we observe in the real world are not one-time stocks immaculately created to be consumed but inventories of "proved reserves," constantly

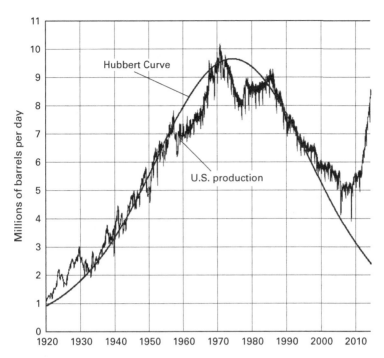

Figure 2.9
Hubbert's curve broken: U.S. crude oil production vs. Hubbert's curve. Jagged line indicates U.S. production (data source: U.S. Energy Information Administration); smooth curve denotes Hubbert's bell curve. MMBPD, millions of barrels per day.

renewed by investment in finding and development. Over time, the investment needed per unit-added is forced up by diminishing returns, and forced down by increasing knowledge. So far, knowledge has prevailed.[3]

Hubbert's model, while working well for studying the life cycle of a particular resource basin over relatively short periods of time when technologies and prices do not vary much, proves to be fatally flawed when extrapolated to world resource supply.

This is not surprising if you consider that while Hotelling focused on the question of optimization of a single mine, Hubbert instead focused on the life cycle of discovery and exhaustion under geological constraints while ignoring intertemporal optimization, or indeed, any

3. M. A. Adelman, H. De Silva and M. F. Koehn, "User Cost in Oil Production," *Resources and Energy* 13 (1991): 217–240.

Tn bbl   2013 $/bbl

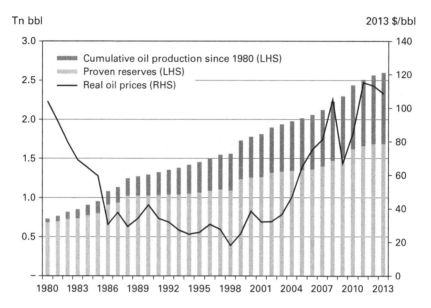

Figure 2.10
World Proven Reserves and Cumulative Production of Oil since 1980.

economic considerations at all. Both models contain core "truths" but also make heroic assumptions that depart greatly from reality.

Industry Cost Curves

Analysts working in the industry often build cost curves in an attempt to summarize the quantities and total costs faced by heterogeneous regions across the world. This is done by stacking up the resource basins according to the amount of production they can achieve on one axis against the breakeven price at which developing the basin becomes economically attractive on the other axis. This seemingly creates a "supply" curve for a resource that compares quantity supplied with price required (figure 2.11).

Industry analysts like to argue that the price of the resource depends on the breakeven cost of that resource basin providing that last marginal unit of resource to meet demand. If prices rise, the next most economical basin would become economical and begin supplying the resource. Until then, it is turned "off." This tacitly assumes that producers myopically produce the moment a price exceeds the breakeven cost and delivers minimum required rates of return on investment.

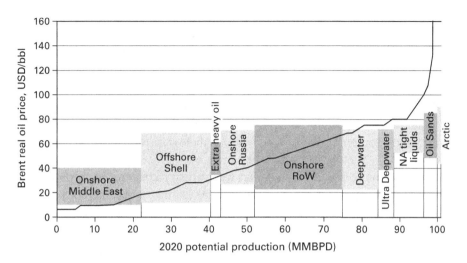

Figure 2.11
Cost of supply curve for global oil, 2020. Future oil prices will be determined by the marginal cost of developing new oil rather than by OPEC interventions. North American shale is expected to outcompete many oil sands and Arctic oil projects. MMBPD, million barrels per day.
Source: UCube by Rystad Energy.

In contrast to Hotelling's and Hubbert's models, it is a bit of a stretch to call this last approach an actual model. Instead, it is more like an accounting of the various fixed and marginal costs faced by producers globally. The industry cost curves approach says nothing about how producers may accelerate or defer production depending on current and expected future prices. As we saw with Hotelling's model, producers may defer production even when prices exceed costs if they know that prices may be even higher in the future. The industry cost curve approach assumes away intertemporal optimization and assumes that producers narrowly focus on immediate profit.

Like Hubbert's model, the industry cost curve approach does acknowledge some of the geological aspects of supply determinants, captured in the differences in breakeven costs between basins. But the cost curve is purely static and, unlike Hubbert's model, says nothing about the life cycle production profile over time.

Additionally, though the cost curve chart tries to summarize the total breakeven costs of production, it somewhat glosses over the fact that for many resource projects, producers face both the initial fixed costs of capital investment and the marginal but continuing costs of operation. Total breakeven costs capture the entire costs of both fixed and marginal costs. But in such circumstances, once a resource project is ready and the fixed cost is sunk, even when prices fall below the breakeven point, all production from existing projects that have already paid fixed costs will continue running as long as prices remain above the marginal costs of production. Hence it is somewhat misleading to imagine that resource basins will immediately "turn on" and "turn off" the moment prices exceed or fall below producers' breakeven costs.

In summary, it can be said that the industry cost curves approach suggests a very static, myopic world. It takes into account geology and rational economic decision making but misses some of the key insights that are included in the other models. It might be better described as a useful accounting exercise that summarizes in one graph the menu of costs faced by potential producers.

Toward a New Theory of Supply

Hotelling's model, Hubbert's model, and the industry cost curves approach all manage to capture some aspects of the reality of the economics of resource supply today, but all also face significant limitations.

Hotelling's central insight is that producers will attempt to optimize production of finite resources intertemporally. The theoretically elegant model can be extended to consider the relaxation of some assumptions, such as heterogeneous costs or market power. But crucially, Hotelling's model relies heavily on the assumptions of perfect control over extraction rates and perfect information about prices, quantities, and costs. These ideal circumstances can be approximated under certain real-life scenarios, such as extraction of a resource from a single storage tank, and to a lesser extent shale fracking. However, Hotelling's model fails to account for the real-life challenges of imperfect information and lack of fine-tuned production control. Hotelling's starkest prediction—his famous rule that prices minus costs should rise exponentially at the discount rate—should not be taken so literally.

Hubbert's logistical model for resource production proves surprisingly good at approximating the life cycle of exploration and development of a single geological basin, when prices are stable and all else remains constant. But when Hubbert's curve is applied across long stretches of time or expanded from a single basin to multiple basins at a national or global scale, its lack of any modeling for economic or technological dynamics becomes increasingly problematic. Its most famous prediction, Hubbert's peak, should also, like Hotelling's rule, not be taken too literally.

Industry cost curves provide a useful snapshot of cost structures across different geological basins at any single point in time. However, this approach is quite static and glosses over important points of Hotelling and Hubbert. Industry cost curves ignore producer intertemporal optimization while considering the various production costs also analyzed by Hotelling, and the life cycle of exploration, development, and depletion analyzed by Hubbert.

All three models afford insight into a particular aspect of the economics of resource supply, but at the expense of abstracting from other complexities, they are in tension with each other. Hotelling's model fails to account for the geological realities of resource extraction, a central tenet of Hubbert's model, by assuming perfect information and perfect control over output. Hubbert's curve features mines following rigid output schedules determined by their particular geology but does not take into account economic optimization or technological progress. Industry cost curves provide a useful static snapshot of diverse costs across various geological basins but feature neither dynamical optimization over time (as in Hotelling's model) nor the geological life cycle (as in Hubbert's model).

At the end of the day, analysts should embrace the insights afforded by each model while recognizing the shortcomings of all three approaches. Only by synthesizing the approaches and understanding when and under what circumstances each model is useful can one approach a more holistic understanding of the economic dynamics of commodity supply.

Mathematical Appendix A: Optimal Control Theory

Optimal control theory was developed in the 1950s and 1960s by Richard Bellman (1920–1984) in the United States and Lev Pontryagin (1908–1988) in the Soviet Union. Optimal control theory is an extension of the standard Lagrangian techniques utilized in the calculus of variations to solve various optimization problems.

In economics, when maximizing the discounted cash flows of a profit stream from an investment project, optimal control problems often take the form

$$\max_{u(t)} \int_0^\infty \pi(x(t),u(t)) e^{-\rho t} dt,$$

where π is the payoff function, $x(t)$ is the state variable, $u(t)$ is the control variable, and ρ is the discount rate. The state variable is controlled by the optimizer through the control variable and needs to follow a "law of motion":

$$\dot{x}(t) = \frac{dx}{dt} = g(x(t),u(t)).$$

For example if $x(t)$ is the quantity of oil in the ground, then $\dot{x}(t) = -u(t)$, the extraction rate. However, $\dot{x}(t)$ could also depend on $x(t)$ itself. For example, such is the case in the optimal control of fisheries, where x will result from both extraction $u(t)$ and the amount of breeding, which itself depends on the size of the stock, $x(t)$.

Traditionally, we would define the Lagrangian as:

$$\mathcal{L} \equiv [\pi(x,u) + \lambda(t)(\dot{x} - g(x,u))]e^{-\rho t},$$

where $\lambda(t)$ is known as the shadow price, which captures the incremental change in the objective function for every unit of change by which the constraint is relaxed or strengthened.

Using the Hamiltonian formulation, we have:

$$\mathcal{H} \equiv \pi(x,u) + \lambda(t)g(x,u).$$

Intuitively, π can be thought of as the instantaneous payoff, λ is the shadow value of "capital" x, and g is the rate of change of capital $\dot{x}$. In other words, the term λg can be thought of as "capital appreciation" and the overall Hamiltonian is the instantaneous value creation at time t. The real underlying economic value of the investment project at any given point in time is the direct payoff the operator gets from the project plus some economic value that comes from increases or decreases in the capital stock according to how the investor is trying to control it:

$$\max_{u(t)} \int_0^\infty \pi(x(t),u(t)) e^{-\rho t} dt = \max_{u(t)} \int_0^\infty \left[\mathcal{H} - (\rho\lambda - \dot{\lambda}x)\right]e^{-\rho t} dt.$$

Obtaining the following first-order conditions:

FOC 1 (optimization over control variable):

$$\frac{\partial \mathcal{H}}{\partial x}\Big|_{u=u^*} = 0.$$

FOC 2 (no arbitrage condition):

$$\frac{\partial \mathcal{H}}{\partial u} - \left(\rho\lambda - \dot{\lambda}\right) = 0,$$

$$-\frac{\partial \mathcal{H}}{\partial u}\Big|_{u=u^*} = \dot{\lambda} - \rho\lambda.$$

The economic intuition behind this first-order condition is that if an investor has a unit of capital or stock worth $\lambda(t)$ that could alternatively be invested in the bank at interest ρ, the "profit" would be $\lambda\rho$ one period later. If instead the investor took the stock and put it into the optimal control problem to "do work," it would increase the problem by one unit of x (i.e., $\frac{\partial \mathcal{H}}{\partial x}$). One period later the initial capital or stock could be resold for $\lambda(t+1)$, yielding a "profit" of

$$\frac{\partial \mathcal{H}}{\partial x} + (\lambda(t+1) - \lambda(t)).$$

To preclude arbitrage between these two investment options, and taking the limit as $t \to 0$, we must have:

$$\rho\lambda(t)dt = \frac{\partial \mathcal{H}}{\partial x}dt + \lambda(t+dt) - \lambda(t),$$

$$-\frac{\partial \mathcal{H}}{\partial u} = \dot{\lambda} - \rho\lambda.$$

When you consider a stock of oil in the ground for example, optimal control theory tells the investor that one need not have to worry about the complexities of the entire investment problem. The investor need only consider how to maximize the value gained from extracting oil (and getting a payoff from that) at each point in time balanced against the capital appreciation gain or loss associated with the fact that with every one barrel of oil extracted the investor loses the shadow value for the amount of oil in the ground. In this case, the shadow price could be thought of as the value of leasing rights.

Hotelling showed that the equilibrium resulting from price-taking firms owning a mine results in the same outcome as a social planner maximizing Marshallian consumer surplus, provided the interest rate used by the firm is equal to the social discount rate.

The problem of a social planner optimizing the output from a single mine, with constant marginal cost c, assuming the total stock of reserves in the mine is finite and known with perfect uncertainty, can be formulated this way:

$$\pi(x(t), u(t)) = \Omega(q(t)) - cq(t),$$

where $\Omega(.)$ is the welfare function, and the control variable $q(t) = -u(t)$ is the extraction rate. The evolution of production is set by the function $g(x(t), u(t)) = -q(t)$, where $x(t)$ is the state variable (the amount of resource remaining in the mine at time t), which is pinned down by the collapsed transversality condition, $x(T) = 0$.

The FOCs are derived as follows:

$$\dot{\Omega}(q(t)) = \lambda(t) + c,$$

$$\dot{\lambda}(t) = \rho\lambda.$$

The second condition can be solved analytically:

$$\lambda(t) = \lambda_0 e^{\rho t}.$$

The first condition shows that marginal welfare must equal the shadow price plus the marginal cost of extraction. The second condition shows that the shadow price changes exponentially at the discount rate ρ, famously known as Hotelling's rule. It argues that the value of the resource extracted today must equal the discounted value of the resource extracted in the future, or else there is suboptimal extraction by the social planner.

For the competitive equilibrium case, we have firms maximizing profit:

$$\pi = p(t)q(t) - cq(t).$$

The FOCs are derived as follows:

$$p(t) = \lambda(t) + c,$$
$$p(t) = c + (p_0 - c)e^{\rho t}.$$

The economic rent from the resource still grows exponentially at the discount rate. Hence, Hotelling showed that the extraction speed of profit-seeking competitive firms replicates the optimization outcome of a social planner trying to optimize Marshallian consumer plus.

Hotelling's insight is that if a company is extracting resources, it needs to think not just about immediate profits but intertemporally. Firms should consider how to maximize not just immediate profit but the whole value of the reserves, taking into account the entire trajectory of prices to the end of the life of the mine.

It should be noted that Hotelling's rule applies to real inflation-adjusted prices, so in nominal terms, the economic rent should be rising at a slower rate of exponential growth or even be constant (if the real interest rate is zero).

Mathematical Appendix B: Hubbert's Logistical Model

The American geologist M. King Hubbert assumed that the cumulative production from a geological area of reserves follows logistic growth:

$$\frac{dQ}{dt} = q = kQ\left(1 - \frac{Q}{Q^\infty}\right),$$

where Q is the cumulative production, q is the instantaneous production, and k and Q^∞ are constants.

The logistical growth model was developed by the Belgian mathematician Pierre François Verhulst (1804–1849) to model self-limiting population growth after Verhulst read the pessimistic assessment *An Essay on the Principle of Population* by the English economist Thomas Malthus (1766–1834).

Hubbert was motivated to follow Verhulst by the intuition that when exploration in a particular geological reserve first begins, the rate of growth of cumulative output rises "almost" exponentially as sweet spots are discovered and engineers gain a better understanding of the geology. However, much like the saturation capacity in a Malthusian world, eventually the reserve begins to exhaust itself as cumulative production approaches Q^∞, which is the ultimately recoverable quantity of reserves, and the rate of growth of cumulative production declines and reverses.

It is important to recognize that Hubbert was not trying to model a single mine. Each single mine may follow some rigid output schedule according to the dictates of geology and mine pressure, but after one aggregates the discoveries and exploitation of multiple mines in a large enough geological area and factors in the learning by doing versus the capacity of the area, the macroscopic pattern begins to mimic that of a logistical curve.

Hubbert's model results in an ordinary differential equation that is easily solved:

$$kdt = \frac{1}{Q\left(1-\dfrac{Q}{Q^\infty}\right)} dQ = \left[\frac{1}{Q} + \frac{1/Q^\infty}{1-\dfrac{Q}{Q^\infty}}\right] dQ.$$

Integrating on both sides, we get:

$$kt + cnst = lnQ - \ln\left(1-\frac{Q}{Q^\infty}\right) = \ln\left(\frac{Q}{1-\dfrac{Q}{Q^\infty}}\right),$$

$$\left(1-\frac{Q}{Q^\infty}\right)Ce^{kt} = Q,$$

$$Ce^{kt} = Q + \frac{Q}{Q^\infty}Ce^{kt} = \left(1+\frac{Ce^{kt}}{Q^\infty}\right)Q,$$

$$Q = \frac{Ce^{kt}}{1+Ce^{kt}/Q^\infty}.$$

This is known as the logistical curve, or sigmoid function, which has a distinctive S shape.

The first derivative, or instantaneous production, creates a bell curve that looks similar to but is not the familiar Gaussian distribution. The Gaussian distribution has tails that decline at rate e^{-x^2}, while the logistical bell curve declines at rate e^{-x}.

3 Fundamentals of Commodity Economics: Demand

In the last chapter we considered various modeling approaches to understanding the economics faced by producers supplying commodities. In this chapter we turn to the demand side of markets, again focusing on energy commodities.

Unlike the history of the study of commodity supply, which can boast of a rich tradition of various modeling approaches that are often in conceptual tension (as seen in the previous chapter), the study of commodity demand tends to be more mundane. One might argue there is a tighter relationship between theory and reality on the demand side, but there is no one-size-fits-all approach to modeling commodity demand either.

Nevertheless, we shall try to sketch out some of the salient features of energy demand and useful modeling approaches, which again should have lessons for commodity demand in general.

Distinguishing Demand Factors by Frequency

It is useful to break down the dynamics of energy demand into the following factors, roughly distinguished by the time frequency of their motion:

1. *Cyclical demand*, driven by price fluctuations and short-term business cycles.
2. *Structural demand*, driven by medium-term factors such as consumer tastes and business investment in efficiency.
3. *Secular demand*, driven by long-term factors such as societal economic development and technological change.

The boundaries of each category, particularly for demand in the medium and long run, are not precise, and that all these factors may be having a simultaneous impact and/or are in opposition to each other.

1. **Short-Term or Cyclical Demand:** In the short run, demand for energy tends to fluctuate owing to changes in prices and macroeconomic business cycles. For instance, holding all else constant, our willingness to go on a long-distance road trip may fall if the price of gasoline rises. Alternatively, a recession that causes a rise in unemployment and hurts consumer purchasing power can compel commuters to prefer taking cheaper public transportation over driving their cars, as occurred during the global recession of 2008–2009.
2. **Medium-Term or Structural Demand:** In the medium term, demand for energy tends to fluctuate as a result of changes in efficiency, business investment, and consumer behavior. For example, high electricity prices may prompt consumers to purchase more expensive but efficient fluorescents and light-emitting diodes (LEDs) over conventional light bulbs. The impact of this investment on demand would outlast the initial price increase that drove the investment.

Consumer tastes can also shift. For example, gas-guzzling SUVs converted from light truck platforms have become popular passenger vehicles. These tastes can also affect the medium-term responsiveness of demand to prices.

3. **Long-Term or Secular Demand:** In the long run, the demand for energy changes owing to economic growth, societal development, and technological advancement. The amount of energy demanded by an economy increases powerfully as it begins to move away from an agrarian focus to one that is based on industries such as cement or steel production, which are highly energy-intensive. But the most advanced economies have shifted to a postindustrial society driven by less energy-intensive services.

In addition, it is important to recognize that all these factors influencing energy demand and prices are in a constant dynamic interaction. For instance, a country's rapid economic growth led by industrial demand for more energy may result in increases in energy prices that feed back into the economy by causing consumers to cut back on driving. Note however how complicated this dynamic can get, as we have not even mentioned the effects of supply side shocks.

Demand Factors by Type of User

Completing this separation by time horizon, we can also divide the components of energy demand by the type of end-user or final consumer. In the United States and other advanced economies, the following five categories typically capture the major sources of energy demand:

1. Transportation demand: the usage of energy to transport people and goods, by cars, trucks, trains, ships, aircraft, etc.
2. Residential demand: energy used by homes and residences
3. Commercial demand: energy used by businesses and commercial properties
4. Industrial demand: energy used by industries and factories
5. Power generation: energy used to generate power for the electricity grid

Figure 3.1 is a graphical flowchart illustration of the broad categories of demand for energy and a detailed breakdown of their respective sources for the advanced economy of the United States in 2015.

This chart brings up several points that are worth considering:

1. Petroleum is currently the dominant source of energy in the transportation sector, while also playing a role in meeting industrial, commercial, and residential demand for energy. It occasionally sees some use for surge power generation (e.g. emergency diesel generators) but oil has largely been phased out of power generation.
2. Power generation is heavily dominated by coal and natural gas, followed by nuclear and renewable energy sources such as solar, wind, and hydro.
3. Natural gas is a versatile energy source used heavily for power generation, as an industrial feedstock, and for heating homes and buildings.
4. Renewable sources (solar, nuclear, hydro, wind, and geothermal) only really feature in power generation, therefore competing with coal and natural gas. However, if electric vehicles continue to rise in popularity, renewable sources may one day displace oil's dominance as the primary energy sources in the transportation sector.
5. A substantial portion of energy generated is actually "rejected"— wasted or unused. According to the U.S. Department of Energy, about 70% of the combustion energy generated in an average

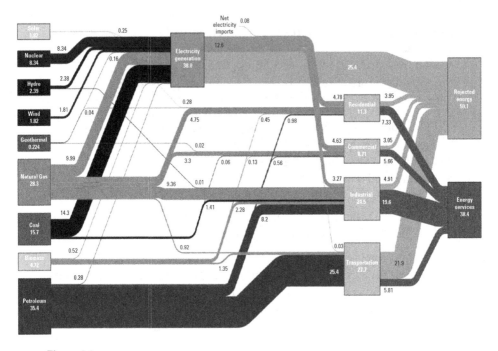

Figure 3.1
Estimated U.S. energy demand in 2015: 97.5 quads.
Source: Lawrence Livermore National Laboratory.

gasoline-powered vehicle is lost internally to engine friction and
exhausted heat. Less than 30% of the energy is actually used to move
the vehicle and its contents.[1] In fact, with so much energy being
lost through wastage, improved energy efficiency can often be the
cheapest option to improve economics of energy supply, as seen in
figure 3.2 which compares the relative costs of energy sources in the
United States. Hence, energy efficiency is sometimes referred to as
the "invisible fuel" or the "fifth fuel."[2]

1. "Where the Energy Goes: Gasoline Vehicles" (Washington, D.C.: U.S. Department
of Energy, Office of Energy Efficiency and Renewable Energy, n.d.) (http://www
.fueleconomy.gov/feg/atv.shtml).
2. "Invisible Fuel," *Economist*, January 17, 2015 (http://www.economist.com/news/
special-report/21639016-biggest-innovation-energy-go-without-invisible-fuel).

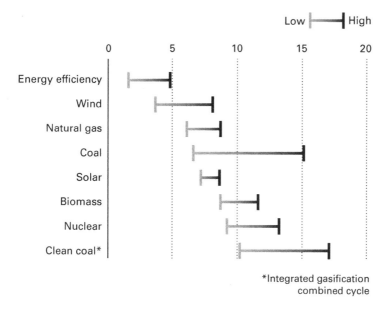

Figure 3.2
Average Energy Costs in the United States, 2009–2014 (cents per kWh).
Improving energy efficiency is the cheapest way to improve energy economics.
Source: American Council for an Energy-Efficient Economy.

Nerlove's Partial Adjustment Model

Now that we have some sense of the primary sources of demand, we turn to how economists can model it. As mentioned earlier, there is no single, one-size-fits-all approach to modeling demand, and analysts should carefully study the market in question to assess what aspects are both important enough to be features in a model.

But most demand models have at least two primary factors affecting the quantity of demand: income and price. Here we discuss in some detail the simplest possible example, Nerlove's partial adjustment model. This model can serve as a foundation for more sophisticated representations of energy demand.[3]

Nerlove's partial adjustment model is first based on a long-term relationship represented by a polynomial function of price and income:

$$D_{t,L} = \alpha P_t^{-\epsilon} Y_t^{\eta},$$

3. Marc Nerlove, "Distributed Lags and Demand Analysis for Agricultural and Other Commodities" (Washington, D.C.: U.S. Department of Agriculture, Agricultural Marketing Service, 1958).

where $D_{t,L}$ is long-term demand, ϵ is the long term price elasticity of demand, and η is the income elasticity of demand.

This polynomial formulation is deliberately chosen this way because, in natural logarithmic terms, this expression becomes linear. By taking natural logs of both sides of the expression, we have the following (where the small capitals represent logarithmic expressions, that is, $d_{t,L} = \ln(D_{t,L})$, etc.):

$$d_{t,L} = \ln(\alpha) - \epsilon p_t + \eta y_t$$

Nerlove's model also assumes actual short-term demand (which is what we actually observe) adjusts toward long-term demand with a lag:

$$\frac{D_{t,L}}{D_{t,S}} = \left(\frac{D_{t,L}}{D_{t-1,S}}\right)^{\delta},$$

where the adjustment term $0 < \delta \leq 1$.

We see that the expression on the right-hand side captures how short-term demand "adjusts" toward the long-term demand depending on the *previous* period's demand and the *current* period's supposed long-term demand.

Solving both equations, we get:

$$d_{t,s} = constant - \epsilon(1-\delta)p_t + \eta(1-\delta)y_{t,s} + \delta d_{t-1,s}.$$

This is a very convenient expression for economists to estimate, for it assumes demand is a log-linear combination of price, income, and one lag of itself. This model can easily be estimated using familiar statistical regression techniques such as ordinary least squares.

More sophisticated versions of demand forecasting often build on this simple structure with more prices, incomes, lags, and other controls in the right-hand side and/or more complicated parameterizations than simple natural logs. But the basic building blocks are all there.

Estimating Short-Term Elasticities

Once the regression is estimated, one can easily back out the price and income elasticities ϵ and η from the slope coefficients. Table 3.1 shows the simple short-term price elasticities of oil calculated for the various countries (from Cooper 2003).[4]

4. John C. B. Cooper, "Price Elasticity of Demand for Crude Oil: Estimates for 23 Countries," *OPEC Review*, 2003, 1–8 (doi:10.1111/1468-0076.00121).

Table 3.1
Estimates of Oil Price Elasticity for Major Industrialized Countries

	Oil consumption growth per capita (%)	Real GDP growth per capita (%)	Price elasticity	
			Short run	Long run
Australia	−0.3	1.7	−0.034	−0.068
Austria	−0.7	3.1	−0.059	−0.092
Canada	−1.3	1.6	−0.041	−0.352
China	3.6	8.6	0.001	0.005
Denmark	−2.5	1.5	−0.026	−0.191
Finland	−1.2	2.1	−0.016	−0.033
France	−1.5	1.7	−0.069	−0.568
Germany	−1.4	1.2	−0.024	−0.279
Greece	2.2	1.5	−0.055	−0.126
Iceland	0.5	2.2	−0.109	−0.452
Ireland	0.2	3.9	−0.082	−0.196
Italy	−0.4	2.2	−0.035	−0.208
Japan	−1.0	8.1	−0.071	−0.357
Korea	8.3	6.4	−0.094	−0.178
Netherlands	−0.5	1.7	−0.057	−0.244
New Zealand	−0.4	1.4	−0.054	−0.326
Norway	0.2	2.9	−0.026	−0.036
Portugal	3.0	2.9	0.023	0.038
Spain	1.3	2.1	−0.087	−0.146
Sweden	1.3	2.8	−0.043	−0.289
Switzerland	−0.7	0.9	−0.03	−0.056
United Kingdom	−1.1	2.0	−0.068	−0.182
United States	−0.7	2.0	−0.061	−0.453

Note: The calculations for China and South Korea are based on the period 1979–2000.

Source: John C. B. Cooper, "Price Elasticity of Demand for Crude Oil: Estimates for 23 Countries," *OPEC Review*, 2003, 1–8 (doi:10.1111/1468-0076.00121).

A rough-and-ready rule of thumb for advanced economies is to assume a long-term (greater than one-year) price elasticity of demand of −0.5 and a short-term (within one year) price elasticity of −0.05. This assumption is generally consistent with the estimates for the advanced economies, in which society has already reached postindustrial levels of energy use. Yet as we can see, in some emerging markets, such as China, elasticity can be problematically estimated as positive. This regression likely captures a period when Chinese oil demand grew strongly for structural reasons associated with economic development despite a rise in oil prices. We will discuss structural factors behind long-term energy demand later in the chapter.

Let us first discuss what a short-term elasticity of -0.05 means. Directly, converting logs into percentages, an elasticity of -0.05 implies a 1 percent increase in prices causes demand to fall by only 0.05 percent within one year. Scaling up, a roughly 200% increase (i.e., a tripling) in prices, is required to cause a mere 10% decline in oil demand within one year! In other words, demand is very *insensitive* to price fluctuations in the short term. Even the longer-term elasticity of 0.5 implies that a 20% permanent increase in prices is necessary to drive about a 10% long-term decline in demand.

This is understandable when one considers the underlying inflexibility of current demand for oil, which again largely stems from oil's use in transportation. The average commuter who uses a personal automobile to commute to her job can hardly stop consuming oil merely because prices at the pump rise. It would likely require selling her car, moving to a new house where public transportation is more accessible, or other costly modifications to switch to a less oil-intensive way of business or life. This demand rigidity explains the very low elasticity of demand to price incentives.

Meanwhile, the adjustment factor δ captures just how sluggishly short-term actual demand approaches the longer-term "desired" demand for oil.

Therefore, for markets to start adjusting to small fluctuations in quantities, very large fluctuations in prices are needed. These extremely small elasticities thus drive the *naturally* high volatility in oil prices as markets adjust to inevitable short-term fluctuations in quantities, which inventories and other mechanisms can only partially mitigate. We should not be surprised that energy prices are so volatile (and we should not be so quick to blame other factors, such as speculation or foreign imports).

Structural Shifts in Energy Demand

The estimates in the table above, as helpful as they are in calculating how much demand should respond to short-term fluctuations in prices, shouldn't blind us to the fact that elasticities themselves may also change over time. On top of cyclical changes in demand, there can also be medium-term structural changes in demand owing to changing tastes.

For example, Hughes, Knittel and Sperling (2008) found that there was a change in short-term price elasticity in U.S. gasoline demand between 1975–1980 and 2001–2006.[5] More specifically, they estimated that the short-run price elasticity decreased from a range of –0.21 to –0.34 for 1975–1980 to a range of –0.034 to 0.077 for 2001–2006. In other words, demand for *gasoline* in the United States. became *less* sensitive to prices during this period as consumers made structural shifts in consumption behavior.

According to the authors, several factors could explain this change. Increased income, for example, can create a wealth effect that stabilizes fuel consumption, regardless of price fluctuations. Improved vehicle efficiency may also make car owners less sensitive to changes in oil prices. Suburban development and the resulting longer daily commutes may have also contributed to higher and more inflexible fuel consumption. Last, an extended period of low real prices of oil spanning the 1990s to early 2000s may have pushed consumers toward making certain irreversible, sticky investment decisions that made adjustment to price fluctuations more costly; that is, they affected the adjustment factor δ.

Secular Energy Demand and Income

We turn now to the last type of demand fluctuation, secular long-term demand changes driven by fundamental transformations in the economy. This demand fluctuation is represented by α or the intercept coefficient in the simple Nerlove model given earlier. Importantly, this factor captures long-term secular changes in demand that wouldn't be accounted for by factors like income and price fluctuations.

We discuss four stylized facts about the relationship between economic growth and energy demand as a country goes through its life cycle of development.

First, in the aggregate, people and economies use more energy as they become wealthier. This is marked by a strong and positive relationship between energy demand per capita and income per capita. Figure 3.3 shows the trajectory in energy demand per capita by country as countries have generally grown richer. Rich economies such as the United States are both richer and consume more energy per capita, though their energy demand tends to flatten out after a certain wealth

5. J. Hughes, C. R. Knittel, and D. Sperling, "Evidence of a Shift in the Short-Run Price Elasticity of Gasoline Demand," *Energy Journal* 29, no. 1 (2008): 113–134.

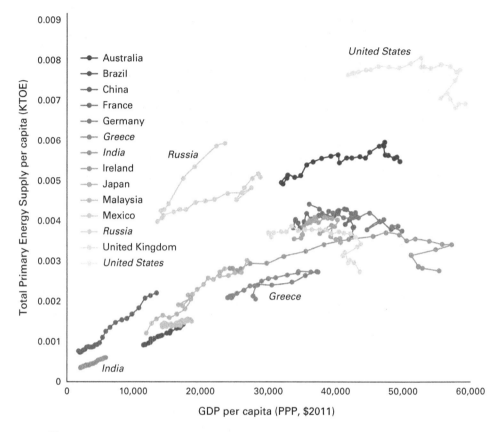

Figure 3.3
Energy Demand and GDP per capita (1990–2014).
Source: International Energy Agency and World Bank.

level is achieved. Meanwhile, emerging economies such as China and India have the potential to grow significantly in terms of energy per capita consumed, in light of how far away they are from achieving advanced economy levels of income.

The second stylized fact is that economies initially become more energy-intensive as they industrialize, and then become more energy-efficient as they modernize and move into services and other postindustrial sectors. (This is sometimes associated with the environmental Kuznets curve, whereby societies first become more polluted as they industrialize, then becomes cleaner as they become wealthy.) In other words, there is a "hump" in the graph of the energy intensity of economies as they develop (energy intensity is defined as the amount of

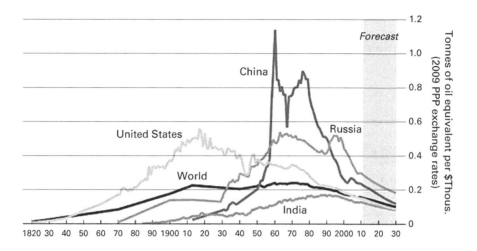

Figure 3.4
Energy intensity per unit of GDP.
Source: BP and the *Economist*.

energy needed to produce one unit of gross domestic product [GDP]).[6] The United States experienced this hump as it transformed from an agrarian society to an industrialized society in the second half of the nineteenth century. U.S. energy intensity peaked in the 1920s, but the country then became less energy-intensive (in GDP terms) throughout the rest of the twentieth century. This decreasing energy intensity accelerated notably in the 1970s–1980s in response to oil shocks.

Interestingly, Russia (and then the Soviet Union) followed a similar pattern as the United States but with a lag of about thirty to fifty years (figure 3.4). There was a sudden spike in energy intensity after the collapse of the Soviet Union, driven more by a plunge in economic output even as energy demand remained stagnant than by a move into energy-intensive sectors.

Finally, China saw the peak of its energy intensity during the Great Leap Forward, when Chinese state planners drove small-scale steel and other extremely energy-intensive activities for a relatively meager

6. Kenneth B. Medlock and Ronald Soligo, "Economic Development and End-Use Energy Demand," *Energy Journal* 22, no. 2 (2001): 77–105.

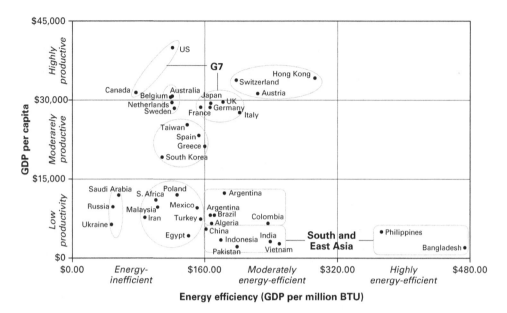

Figure 3.5
GDP vs. energy efficiency (top forty economies by GDP, 2004).
Source: World Bank.

economic output. This situation was reversed only in the 1980s following the "Four Modernizations" (of agriculture, industry, science, and
technology), when the Chinese economy surpassed Russia's in energy
efficiency and began approaching world levels (see figure 3.4).

The third stylized fact is that there is considerable variation in energy
usage among countries. Even though rich countries are more productive, they are not necessarily more energy-efficient. Countries that are
well endowed with energy resources (e.g., Saudi Arabia, Russia) tend
to be less efficient as a result of cheaper or even subsidized domestic
energy prices (figure 3.5).

The final stylized fact is that a certain minimum amount of energy
appears to be essential for basic human needs and development. Figure
3.6 shows how rapidly one's quality of life (as measured by the UN's
Human Development Index) can fall off once an economy falls below
a certain minimum level of energy consumption (about 4 GWh per
annum). Energy is a basic means to improve the lives of people, which
is why it is one of the main objectives of economic development and
foreign aid.

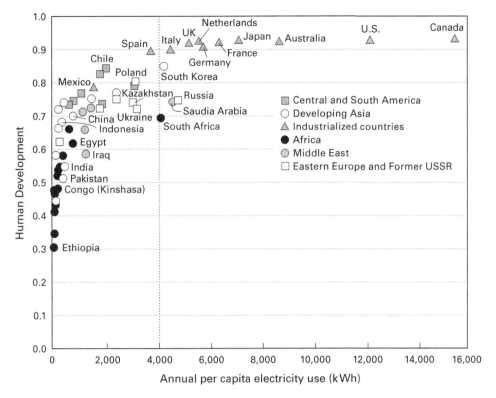

Figure 3.6
Human Development Index vs. per capita electricity use. The Human Development Index, a measurement of human well-being, reaches its maximum plateau at about 4,000 KWh of annual electricity use per capita. Sixty nations are plotted, representing 90% of Earth's population.
Source: S. Benka, *Physics Today*, April 2002, p. 39, adapted from A. Pasternak, Lawrence Livermore National Laboratory Report UCRL-ID-140-773.

Bringing Demand and Supply Together: Equilibrium in Theory and Practice

Now that we have discussed approaches to understanding both commodity demand and supply, it is time to bring them altogether. It would seem obvious that supply has to equal demand for there to be equilibrium. Economists call this the market-clearing condition.

In theory, the market-clearing condition sets equilibrium prices in such a fashion as to exactly incentivize the right amount of both demand and supply, and everyone lives happily ever after.

In practice, however, energy demand and supply are part of a constantly changing and complex system. Supply constantly adjusts to fluctuations in price, medium-term investments, geopolitical events, new geological discoveries, and technological progress. For instance, the shale revolution in the United States and subsequently in other parts of the world warrants a recalculation of optimal levels of extraction under the Hotelling model.

On the other hand, demand has to adjust to short-term business cycles, price fluctuations, and technological progress, as well as changing consumer preferences and economic growth. Note how many factors simultaneously affect both supply and demand here)

Nevertheless, the main thread connecting the dynamics of demand and supply is price. Hence price is the key engine and information-aggregating indicator capturing a multiplicity of commodity market dynamics.

How has the price of commodities evolved over time? Hotelling's rule would say prices should rise at the rate of interest to incentivize current production. Hubbert does not having anything to say about price directly but predicts "peak resource," which presumably means prices also need to rise as supply continues to fall once.

But looking at the history of resource markets, one could argue that in the very long term, the price of commodities eventually declines to zero, in defiance of all the theories. As technological progress brings better substitutes to the market at more competitive prices, the economic relevance of a commodity declines over time and is eventually eclipsed by that of another commodity.

For example, whale oil was once among the most valuable commodities on the planet, and the majestic creatures were hunted almost to extinction in the pursuit of the precious commodity. Now whale oil is practically worthless because society has found a technological substitute: petroleum.

Technological progress and the maturation of the refining industry, pioneered by John D. Rockefeller, whose Standard Oil (today's ExxonMobil) promised a high-quality "standard" for refined petroleum, allowed humans to refine the hitherto smelly and dangerous "rock oil" into refined petroleum with properties that matched or exceeded those of whale oil at a fraction of the cost (figure 3.7).

Indeed, history is littered with commodities once considered invaluable for economic or strategic reasons but that are now mundane and ubiquitous at best or ignored at worst, thanks to technological progress.

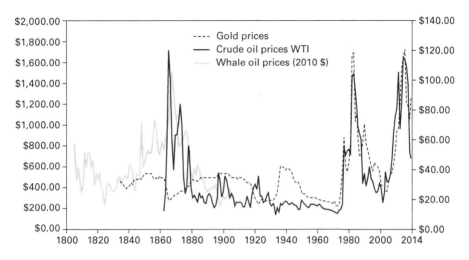

Figure 3.7
Whale oil, crude oil, and gold prices, 1800–2014.

Wars were fought over commodities that wouldn't get a second look today. The wars over the sugar islands of the Caribbean were mentioned earlier. During the Napoleonic Wars, the Royal Navy under Horatio Nelson burned Copenhagen to retain British access to the critical timber and hemp resources in the Baltic. Japan invaded British Malaysia and the Dutch East Indies (modern Indonesia) in part for their valuable natural rubber plants. Interestingly, today synthetic rubber supplies almost all needs. The legacies of strategic commodities can still crop up in surprising places. The United States still maintains a strategic helium reserve, forcing NASA to buy from it at inflated prices a commodity that is cheaply put in children's balloons worldwide.

Commodity Supercycles

But while commodity prices eventually go to zero, the process may take centuries or more. Within the span of a human lifetime, commodity prices often gyrate between high and low levels in so-called supercycles. Figure 3.7 shows how oil prices jumped to over $100 per barrel in the 1860s, only to fall back by the 1890s. Prices spiked again in 1973, fell back in 1986, rose again in the 2000s, and fell back in 2014.

Figure 3.8 shows wheat prices since 1657. Again, the general trend is downward as increased transportation efficiency facilitated world trade and made crop specialization economical in the late nineteenth

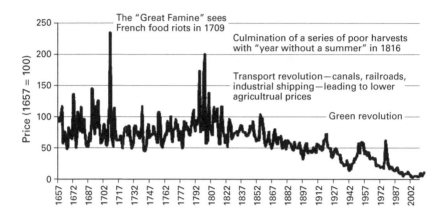

Figure 3.8
Real wheat prices, 1657–2005.
Source: SG Cross Asset Research, GFD.

century. More recently, since the 1950s, the so-called green revolution has introduced fertilizers and specialized strains of seeds that have dramatically increased crop yields and agricultural productivity. And despite fears over recent food price spikes, the world may very well be on the cusp of a green revolution 2.0 with the introduction of new genetic techniques that promise another era of improvements in agricultural yields.

But food prices, like oil prices, have also seen large spikes and supercycles. These might be aberrations in the long-term downward trend, but they were certainly eventful to the people living in it. Indeed, many political revolutions have occurred around these price cycles, from the French Revolution to the modern Arab Spring.

Yet in all price supercycles upward, the seeds of its eventual decline are sown. High prices foment economic weakness and political instability, but they also ration demand and incentivize investment in new supply and technological search for alternatives that eventually bring prices back down. Figure 3.9 is a stylized diagram capturing this supercycle between high and low prices.

This supercycle dynamic also works on the downside as well, as low prices and ample supply stimulate rapid and often wasteful demand, while deterring the investment needed to ensure future supply. This dynamic again establishes the conditions for another episode of surging prices.

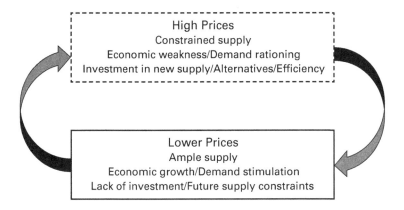

Figure 3.9
The price supercycle.

Ideally, far-sighted investors should make the investments to ensure that supply is available before prices need to spike, but unfortunately, the investment cycle for most commodities is not a smooth process. The substantial amount of uncertainty and time lags between investment and production makes the seamless linkage of future demand and future supply a rather lumpy and imprecise one. The world economy is likely to be plagued by commodity price supercycles for the foreseeable future.

Conclusion

This chapter discussed the main factors behind resource demand, focusing again on energy as a representative example. We discussed the various factors—cyclical, structural, and secular—that can drive demand in the short, medium, and long term. Then we combined these factors with our earlier insights on supply to discuss how demand and supply meet to form a market-clearing price equilibrium, something cleaner in theory than in practice.

While the complicated dance among demand, supply, and prices often results in jarring supercycles of high and low prices, ultimately technology is the champion, and the commodities we study in this book may one day be consigned to the dustbin of history and replaced by new ones.

Module II: Financial Markets for Commodities

Module I covered the underlying fundamentals of demand and supply and how they drive market price dynamics. In this module we turn to the associated market for financial instruments that are linked to the physical markets for commodities.

In chapter 4 we discuss the basic instruments that exchange price risk between financial participants. We discuss the structure of spot contracts, futures contracts, and options, including the famous Black-Scholes-Merton pricing model for European call options.

In chapter 5 we turn to the financial participants themselves and their motivations for entering the market for financial instruments. We discuss hedging, or the offloading of physical risk onto counterparties, and speculation, or the assumption of commodity price risk for alpha return outperformance.

Chapter 6 concludes with a simple model of price discovery that puts all the pieces together to show how the physical spot market, the storage market, and the financial market are linked.

4   Fundamentals of Commodity Derivatives

Introduction

The first three chapters of this book discussed the fundamentals of commodity economics. We analyzed the factors and modeling approaches for producers who supply and consumers who demand commodities.

In this chapter we turn to the world of financial contracts and derivatives linked to commodities, which aid in the transaction and allocation of risk between market participants. We begin with a brief reintroduction to the broad categories of financial derivatives associated with commodities market. We then examine the factors that influence the pricing of these assets. Subsequently we delve into understanding the categories of participants in the commodity derivatives market and their reasons for hedging and speculation. A discussion of options and how to value them concludes the chapter.

Spot Contracts and Forward (Futures) Contracts

Two basic types of contracts form the backbone of commodities markets and how they function. These are spot contracts and forward or futures contracts:

1. **Spot Contracts:** A spot contract or a spot transaction is simply the purchase or sale of a commodity for exchange immediately (or at most, a few days after the trade date). The exchange happens "on the spot." Most market transactions, such as the typical purchase of goods at a supermarket, can be thought of as spot transactions. The spot market for commodities is no different. Throughout the rest of the chapter, we will use the designation S_t to denote the spot price at time t.

2. **Forward (Futures) Contracts:** A forward contract on a commodity is a contract between a buyer and a seller in which the seller promises delivery to the buyer of a standardized quantity and quality of a commodity at a *predetermined price* and a set time in the future. The predetermined nature of the price is the most important characteristic of a forward contract. For example, the holder of a one-year forward contract would pay the preset price of $100 for the guaranteed delivery of a barrel of oil *one year in the future*, regardless of the spot price of oil one year in the future. The predetermined price distinguishes a forward contract from a spot contract, in which the exchange happens immediately at the market price.

Because commodities are fungible, one can specify only a standardized amount of quantity of the commodity without being too specific as to its origin. This distinguishes commodities from other financial assets, such as corporate equities or mortgage-backed securities, where the assets can be heterogeneous (e.g., company stock prices obviously vary with the company, and some are far more valuable than others).

A futures contract is very similar to a forward contract. The difference lies in the context of the market relationship in which the contract is traded. Forward contracts can be private contracts negotiated directly, often through a preexisting commercial relationship. This arrangement is known as an "over-the-counter" agreement. By contrast, futures contracts are traded on an impersonal exchange (e.g., the New York Mercantile Exchange or the Chicago Board of Trade) and typically are standardized to certain delivery dates, quantity, and quality parameters. Exchanges also require participants to maintain minimum levels of capital to ensure every transaction can be smoothly processed. Traders of futures contracts rarely meet each other as the exchange intermediates the transaction.

Regardless, forward and futures contracts are identical in their primary economic characteristic, namely, the forward or future price F_t^T of the commodity set at the time of contract (t) for delivery at some point in the future ($T > t$). We will use the two terms more or less interchangeably throughout the rest of the chapter.

Types of Spot and Futures Market Behavior

The relationship between spot and futures contracts is complex, and the shape of the entire spot/futures price curve when graphed can reveal much about market conditions. There are generally two ways in which the spot and futures markets can behave: in backwardation or in contango.

1 Backwardation

When the futures price of a commodity is lower than its spot price, or $F_t^{t+1} \leq S_t$, the market is said to be in *backwardation*. In other words, the pre-determined price of a commodity for delivery in the future, based on all available information today, is *lower* than the price the market asks for immediate delivery.

Backwardation is often a sign of a temporarily tight market condition. Supplies may be temporarily disrupted (e.g., a hurricane might disrupt the usual supply of gasoline) or demand unusually high (e.g., for ice during a heat wave). Traders are willing to pay a premium for immediate delivery. But in the future, the market may expect demand to cool down or supply to return to normal, so the futures price is lower than the spot price.

2 Contango

Conversely, when the futures price of an asset is higher than its spot price, or $F_t^{t+1} \geq S_t$, the market is said to be in *contango*. Contango often signifies a loose market in which immediate supply is plentiful and traded at a discount. If the commodity is not sold in a spot market, it must be stored before it can be sold in the next period, meaning the future price will need to be higher to take into account the storage costs. On the other hand, there may be value in having an immediate supply at hand, called the convenience yield, which we will discuss later.

As figures 4.1a and 4.1b show, analysts typically graph the relationship between time and prices of the various futures contracts over their various delivery dates, with the spot price at the very front. This "futures curve" makes the state of the futures market immediately and visually intuitive. A downward-sloping futures curve indicates backwardation, while an upward-sloping futures means contango. In practice, it is not unknown to see one portion of the curve in contango and another portion in backwardation.

Analysts and economists study the futures curve carefully not only because the curve says something about current market conditions but also because futures prices can be used as a market signal of what the market thinks future spot prices will be. (Note the rather confusing

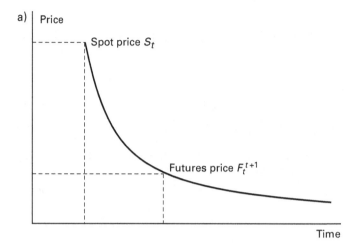

Figure 4.1a
Backwardation.

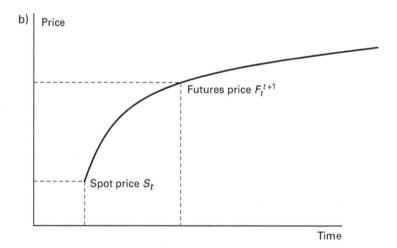

Figure 4.1b
Contango.

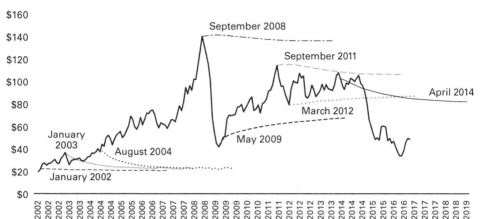

Figure 4.2
Crude oil futures prices and spot prices, January 2002–May 2019.
Source: Bloomberg.

distinction: the futures price versus the spot price in the future or the *future* spot price.) After all, if the futures price says a buyer/seller is willing to pay/receive $100 today for a barrel of oil tomorrow, wouldn't that be because both the buyer and seller thinks the *spot* price tomorrow will be approximately $100? As we will see in the discussion of risk premia later in the chapter, this is not quite the case, but it's not a bad starting point.

And indeed, many companies and organizations (including the U.S. government) use futures prices as a prediction of future spot prices. Figure 4.2 shows the history of spot oil prices since 2002, with the futures curve shown for certain times linked to the spot price at the time. The figure shows how the futures curve can be reasonably accurate about the future direction of spot prices but does a rather terrible job of predicting what that future spot price will actually be. Futures curves routinely underestimate how volatile spot prices can actually be.

Who Is "the Market"?

Next we turn to the types of market participants who decide to trade spot and forward or futures contracts. While their origin can be diverse, market participants can be compartmentalized into two

distinct groups: hedgers, or "commercial" participants, and speculators, or "non-commercial" participants.

Hedgers, or "Commercial" Participants: Hedgers are generally
physical market participants with significant outside income or
expenses linked to the price of the underlying asset who wish to
offload risk by taking a counteracting position. For instance, a wheat
farmer may want to reduce risk around his expected crop income by
locking in the price for his wheat. He will do this by selling wheat
futures, which guarantees he can sell his wheat at a certain price.
Conversely, an airline may want to reduce risk around its jet fuel
expenses by locking in the price for fuel by buying jet fuel forward
contacts. In both cases, they are classic hedgers who wish to buy
(or go "long") or sell (go "short") forward or futures contracts in
light of their natural position in the underlying commodity, and are
motivated to reduce their price exposure. They are sometimes called
"commercial" participants because they have physical commercial
operations linked to the price of the commodity.

Speculators, or "Noncommercial" Participants: Speculators are
defined as participants who do not have a direct income or physical
business risk associated with the underlying commodity. Instead, they
enter into contracts believing they have superior information about
market conditions and can arbitrage to make money. For example, a
speculator might believe that his weather forecast model is predicting
a sharp cold front approaching that hasn't been priced into natural gas
prices. The speculator would then buy natural gas futures today in the
hopes that by the time the cold front hit, he would be able to sell his
natural gas at a spot price higher than his purchase price and pocket
the difference as profit.

In practice, the line between a speculator and a hedger can be
blurred. An asset manager may own a single storage tank in Louisiana
and claim that its operations are those of a hedger, when in truth its
purely financial operations exceed its physical operations significantly.
Conversely, large upstream oil companies that have a genuine need to
hedge may possess large trading operations whose speculative profits
are an integral part of the company's business model. Furthermore,
there are examples of large commercial entities with massive exposure
to commodities that nevertheless strategically choose not to hedge at
all, such as ExxonMobil and Saudi Aramco. In practice, the noncommercial share of outstanding positions in the U.S. oil futures market is

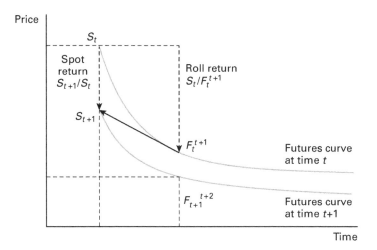

Figure 4.3
Dividing a Rolling Strategy Return into the Spot Return and the Roll Return.

typically larger than the commercial share.[1] We'll dive deeper into the rationales for hedging or not later.

Risk Premia and Risk Neutrality

A critically important feature of futures prices is that they can contain information about expected future spot prices. Indeed, any systematic deviation of futures prices (F_t^T) from expected future spot prices ($E_t(S_T)$) can be arbitraged by speculators. This spread is known as the risk premium.

Consider a risk-neutral speculator who adopts a simple rolling strategy of buying one-period-ahead futures contract at F_t^{t+1}, waiting until expiration at time $t+1$, and selling the commodity at the future spot price, S_{t+1}. Regardless of the risk involved in adopting such an investment strategy, this method would systemically earn money on average (also known as generating alpha) if the market is consistently in backwardation such that the futures price is less than the next period's spot price: $F_t^{t+1} \leq S_{t+1}$ (see figure 4.3). The solid line in figure 4.3 shows the return to this buy-and-hold strategy, which in turn can be divided into

---

1. Kenneth B. Medlock III and Amy Myers Jaffe, "Who Is in the Oil Futures Market and How Has It Changed?," (Rice University, James Baker Institute for Public Policy, August 6, 2009) (http://bakerinstitute.org/media/files/news/94bb2e2c/EF-pub-MedlockJaffe OilFuturesMarket-082609.pdf).

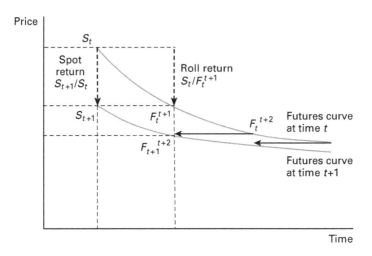

Figure 4.4
Futures and Expected Future Spot Prices without Risk Premia.

the two dotted lines, the spot return, $\dfrac{S_{t+1}}{S_t}$, and the inverse of the roll

return, $\dfrac{F_t^{t+1}}{S_t}$. Mathematically, $\dfrac{S_{t+1}}{F_t^{t+1}} = \dfrac{S_{t+1}}{S_t} * \left(\dfrac{F_t^{t+1}}{S_t} \right)^{-1}$.

Likewise, if the futures price were always systemically higher than the future spot price, $F_t^{t+1} \geq S_{t+1}$ (i.e., in contango), then the risk-neutral arbitrageur could take the opposite approach by selling futures contracts. The arbitrageur would buy from the spot market in the next period and deliver to the futures contract buyer at the predetermined price, which would always be higher, resulting in pure profit.

Clearly, this strategy would not be sustainable because once it became known (assuming perfect information in markets), an infinite number of arbitrageurs would take infinitely large long or short positions in the futures contract. This process would force the futures price to converge to the market expectation of the future spot price: $F_t^{t+1} = E_t(S_{t+1})$, as shown in figure 4.4. The spot return and the inverse roll return would exactly cancel each other out.

Hence, under the assumptions of an infinite depth of risk-neutral speculators and no systematic arbitrage opportunities, futures prices are indeed the market expectation of future spot prices. Here, futures prices are indeed a reasonable indicator of the future trajectory of spot prices. The roll return would be exactly the inverse of the expected spot return and on average, they would cancel each other out and the alpha from the rolling strategies described above would on average be zero.

However, there is some evidence that markets are not perfectly risk neutral and there is alpha to be picked up as a result of embedded risk premia, as people need compensation for taking risk. We return to this situation in chapter 8 on commodity alpha.

For now, we discuss theories as to why futures prices might deviate systematically away from expected future spot prices (i.e., there is a risk premium), and in doing so develop a better understanding of the broader structure of the futures curve and its relationship with the behavior of market participants. These two theories are the Keynes-Hicks theory of hedging pressure, or "normal backwardation," and the Working-Kaldor theory of storage.

Keynes-Hicks Theory of Hedging Pressure

By now you might be wondering where risk premia come from. They come from counterparties, such as physical producers or consumers wanting to hedge their price risk. These counterparties are willing to pay a premium in return for transferring such risk to financial investors.

This insight was formalized by British economists John Maynard Keynes (1883–1946) and John Hicks (1904–1989), who argued that producers typically have a more substantial share of income linked to commodity prices than consumers. For instance, a wheat farmer is particularly fearful of a drop in wheat prices (and thus has a stronger incentive to hedge his income by selling his crops forward) because almost his entire income hinges on that price. By comparison, the average consumer—say, a worker who buys wheat bread for breakfast every day—is conversely afraid of a rise in wheat prices, but probably not as fearful as the farmer is of an equal magnitude fall. After all, the consumer's breakfast bread probably constitutes a smaller share of his income. As a result, Keynes and Hicks argued, *sellers* have a greater need to hedge prices than their consuming counterparts. This "hedging pressure" is what forces sellers to be willing to sell their produce at a discount below the expected future price, for their peace of mind.

This discount of the futures prices below the expected future spot price in turn attracts speculators willing to take on the risk of a sudden drop in future wheat prices in return for some expected gain. Since spot

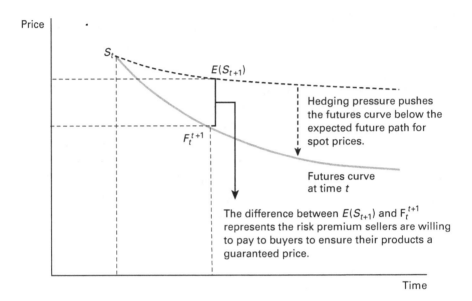

Figure 4.5
Normal Backwardation.

prices tend to be stationary, futures prices that are lower than expected future spot prices will generally drive backwardation in the futures curve, as shown in figure 4.5. This causes the phenomenon Keynes and Hicks called *normal backwardation*.

Keynes and Hicks argued that commodity markets should typically be backwardated, but we can consider a similar argument for "normal contango," which might occur when there are "natural consumers" who have a greater incentive to hedge their purchase prices than producers. For example, an airline company concerned about a potential rise in jet fuel costs may choose to hedge by purchasing petroleum product futures and pay a higher premium than expected spot prices to guarantee a ceiling to its fuel costs.

This consistent difference between futures prices and expected future spot prices is the risk premium. It can be considered the economic equivalent to the "insurance commission" paid by physical hedgers to speculators to assume the risk of the offsetting financial position. The distinction between physical hedgers and speculators in the trading behavior is explored in greater depth later in the chapter.

Working-Kaldor Theory of Storage

The Keynes-Hicks hedging pressure spot markets and futures markets can interact with each other. Another way that spot markets and futures markets can interact is through the economics of storage for commodities. This theory was first developed by the American economist Holbrook Working (1895–1985) and the Hungarian British economist Nicholas Kaldor (1908–1986).[2]

In essence, storage is a technology that allows one to transfer a physical supply from the past to the future, in this way creating another link between the spot market and the futures market. Three key factors drive a storage operator's decision making:

1. **Storage cost** (c_t), which is sometimes assumed to be proportional to the value of the underlying commodity. For instance, storing natural gas in depleted reservoirs entails pumping in a permanent amount of "cushion gas" to maintain adequate pressure and deliverability rates.
2. **Convenience yield** (κ_t), which captures the economic value of the optionality of having immediate supplies of the commodity at hand (real optionality is discussed in a later chapter). This value can be positive or negative. If there is so much supply that there is nowhere to store the commodity, the storage operator might end up paying the buyer to take the commodity away from him (perhaps in the form of a discount).
3. **Risk-free interest rate** $(1 + r_t^f)$, which captures the opportunity cost of not selling the commodity in the present period and saving it elsewhere to earn a small, riskless return. This is also known as the "cost to carry."

To better illustrate the decision-making process, let's consider an example of a storage operator who faces a simple market with a spot price of S_t and a futures contract for delivery at time $t + 1$ at price F_t^{t+1}, to be paid at $t + 1$. Suppose the cost of financing or the risk-free rate of interest at time t is r_t^f. Suppose the cost of storage is a proportional c_t and the convenience yield is proportional κ_t.

Let's consider first the scenario where the commodity curve is in contango, that is, $F_t^{t+1} \geq S_t$. We can show how storage arbitrage imposes an upper bound on how far the futures curve can exceed the spot

2. Holbrook Working, "Theory of the Inverse Carrying Charge in Futures Markets," *Journal of Farm Economics* 30 (1948): 1–28; Nicholas Kaldor, "Speculation and Economic Stability," *Review of Economic Studies* 7 (1939): 1–27.

curve—an upper bound on how deeply the futures curve can be in contango. The storage operator can borrow S_t at interest r_t^f and buy one unit of the commodity on the spot market. Then he can store this unit at cost $-c_t S_t$; he may also be in a position to earn the convenience yield $+\kappa_t S_t$. He can then commit to sell the stored commodity for a price F_t^{t+1}. At time $t + 1$, he must repay his loan with interest $\left(1 + r_t^f\right) S_t$. To prevent risk-free arbitrage, the profit from this strategy must be less than or equal to zero:

$$F_t^{t+1} - c_t S_t + \kappa_t S_t - \left(1 + r_t^f\right) S_t \le 0.$$

Thus we have an upper bound on the futures price, or in other words a maximum degree of possible contango:

$$\left. F_t^{t+1} \right|_{contango} \le \left(1 + r_t^f + c_t - \kappa_t\right) S_t.$$

However, this inequality holds only as long as there is sufficient storage capacity to accept another unit of the commodity. Under conditions of full storage capacity, the cost of storage becomes effectively infinite and futures prices may rise further, beyond any upper bound, pushing the market into extreme contango.

Now let's consider a scenario where the commodity curve is in backwardation: $F_t^{t+1} \le S_t$. Again, we show how storage arbitrage imposes a soft lower bound on how far the futures price can fall below current spot prices.

The storage operator may decide to immediately sell one unit of the commodity at price S_t. He can invest the proceeds of this sale at interest r_t^f. The storage operator may also be in a position to reap the economic benefit of no longer having to pay storage costs $c_t S_t$ but may also suffer the lost convenience yield $\kappa_t S_t$. He would also commit to risklessly replenishing his inventories by purchasing a futures contract at price F_t^{t+1}. Again, to prevent risk-free arbitrage, the profit from this strategy must be less than or equal to zero:

$$\left(1 + r_t^f\right) S_t + c_t S_t - \kappa_t S_t - F_t^{t+1} \le 0.$$

Similar to the contago scenario, we have a lower bound on the futures price, or a maximum degree of possible backwardation:

$$\left. F_t^{t+1} \right|_{backwardation} \ge \left(1 + r_t^f + c_t - \kappa_t\right) S_t.$$

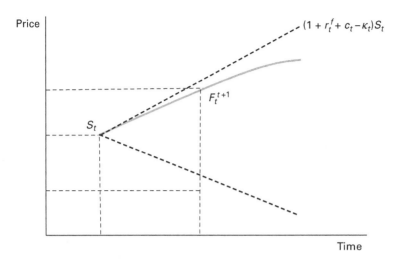

Figure 4.6
Upper and lower bounds to degree of contango and backwardation.

Correspondingly, this inequality can hold only if inventories are not depleted and there remains one unit of commodity to sell on spot markets immediately. If inventories are exhausted, then this inequality may also break down and futures prices may drop further below this lower bound, pushing the market into extreme backwardation. Notice that these two scenarios create an upward and downward boundary for the futures curve, as in figure 4.6.

Under conditions in which both inequality relationships hold, then we have equality and the following relationship, which also serves as a definition of convenience yield:

$$F_t^{t+1} = \left(1 + r_t^f + c_t - \kappa_t\right)S_t.$$

In practice, this defined convenience yield can be challenging to realize owing to market imperfections such as transaction costs, uncertainty, and the like.

Before we conclude this section, let's see what happens if we abstract away from both storage costs (which may be applicable for a producer facing an optimal extraction problem, as storage is effectively free) and convenience yields.

Then we have:

$$F_t^{t+1} = \left(1 + r_t^f\right)S_t.$$

Under conditions of risk neutrality or no uncertainty, $F_t^{t+1} = E_t[S_{t+1}]$. Then our equation becomes the same Hotelling's rule we saw earlier, which posits that expected spot prices should rise at the risk-free rate of interest:

$$E_t[S_{t+1}] = \left(1 + r_t^f\right)S_t.$$

We have rederived Hotelling's rule of optimal extraction from the Kaldor-Working theory of storage.

Options

We need to consider a final set of derivatives known as options. Options are used not just for commodities but for a wide set of asset classes. Other textbooks go into option theory in more depth; here we will sketch out some of the basic concepts, as they are useful for commodity traders as well, and some of the theory on *valuing* options we will return to later, in chapter 6.

Unlike a futures contract, an option contract gives the contract holder the *right* but not the *obligation* to buy (referred to as a "call" option) or sell (referred to as a "put" option) an asset at a preset price in the future. Like the difference between futures and forward contracts, standardized options are traded on exchanges while nonstandardized options are traded over-the-counter and are not publicly listed.

The simplest form of option is the European call option. This option allows the buyer or holder to buy (or go long on) the underlying asset at a certain strike price to be exercised at a predetermined time. Because there is also a functioning spot market, the option would only be exercised when it is "in the money," meaning that the spot price is higher than the strike price. Otherwise, there is no incentive to exercise the option since the holder can purchase the commodity more cheaply at the spot price. In this case, the option expires at the time of its maturity.

Mathematically, buying or going long a European call option has the payoff profile shown in the top left-hand corner of figure 4.7a and stated thus:

$$V_{long\ call}\left(S(T), T\right) = \max\left(S(T) - K, 0\right).$$

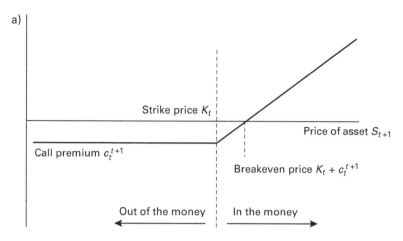

Figure 4.7a
A long position on a call option.

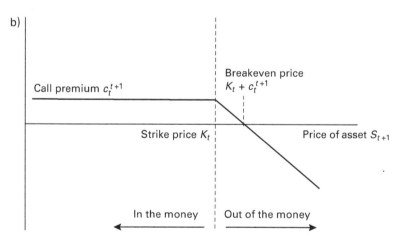

Figure 4.7b
A short position on a call option.

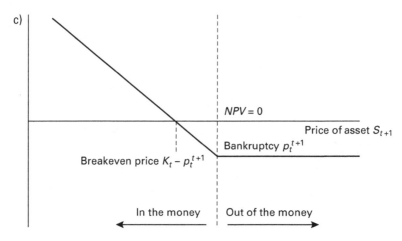

Figure 4.7c
A long position on a put option.

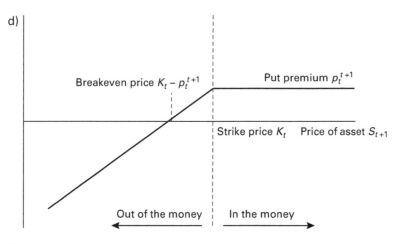

Figure 4.7d
A short position on a put option.

Similarly, holding a put option allows the buyer or holder the right to sell an underlying asset at a certain strike price at a predetermined time. A put option has the payoff profile as shown in figure 4.7c and is valued as such:

$$V_{long\ put}\left(S(T),T\right)=\max\left(K-S(T),0\right).$$

Investors can also sell or underwrite options, which have an opposite payoff profile (graphically represented by a reflection of the profit profile across the x-axis, as in figures 4.7b and 4.7d). They have the following payoff profiles:

$$V_{Short\ call}\left(S(T),T\right)=\min\left(K-S(T),0\right).$$

$$V_{Short\ put}\left(S(T),T\right)=\min\left(S(T)-K,0\right).$$

The prices of both call and put options are also known as option *premia*, and the spot price at which the option is worth more than zero is known as the *breakeven* price.

The contingent nature of an option means that the value of holding an option *increases* as the volatility of the price of the underlying asset increases. Typically, investors dislike risk, but options holders prefer it. Options holders always have downside protection, while the upside potential always exists up until the point of maturity.

Let's consider the example of an investor holding a European call option that will mature in a day's time. The strike price is $90 while the price of the underlying asset is $89 (the option is out of the money). If the price of the underlying asset falls by $2, the option will not be exercised and the payoff is zero. However, if the price of the underlying asset increases by $2, the option will be in the money and will pay out $1. But what if the variance is much higher? If the price of the underlying asset falls by $5, the payoff will still be zero. However, if the price of the underlying asset increases by $5, the payoff will be $4. The investor should not care about any downside risk. The same intuition holds even when the option is deep in the money at the beginning. Of course, this downside protection comes at the cost of paying the call option premium at the beginning.

Implied Volatility

Since the value of the option increases as the volatility of the price of the underlying commodity increases, one could also infer the expected volatility of the price by analyzing the price of the option. If the prices of the premia for the options are low, the market is implying that there is low volatility for the security. If, on the other hand, the prices of the option premia are high, then the market is implying high volatility for the security. Thus the options market opens up a platform where traders can recognize what the market believes to be the volatility of the underlying asset. Should a trader feel that this implied volatility of the share price of a particular stock in the market is less than what she believes it should be, she will choose to take up long option positions. Inadvertently, this unique attribute of options has added new layers of depth to financial markets, as investors can now express their views about the volatility of the asset and not just the direction of its spot price.

Put-Call Parity

The prices of put and call options with the same underlying asset, maturities, and strike prices are tightly bound to each other in a relationship known as put-call parity. This stems from the facts that (1) the payoff profile of an option can be replicated by holding or short selling a combination of stock and a risk-free bond, and (2) the payoff profile from owning a share and a put option (at a particular strike price = K) is equal to owning a risk free bond (with face value = K) and a call option (again, with a strike price = K).

Thus, in a perfect, efficient capital market, where there can be no arbitrage opportunities, the value of a portfolio with a share and a put option should be equal to the value of a portfolio with a risk-free bond and a call option.

$$C(t,K) - P(t,K) = S(t) - K.B(t,T),$$

where $B(t,T)$ refers to the present value of a risk-free zero-coupon bond with a par value of $1 and maturity at time T.

This equality further suggests that if one were to know any three of the prices of a call option, put option, zero-coupon bond, or stock, one could solve for the price of the fourth.

Valuing Options

The put-call parity establishes a static relationship between call options and put options of similar maturity and strike price. However, it does not allow us to value an option directly based on its own characteristics. Financial economists have therefore introduced a more sophisticated architecture for options pricing.

In 1900 the French mathematician Louis Bachelier first proposed a model of the movement of stock prices using stochastic Brownian motion.[3] Brownian motion was named in honor of the Scottish botanist Robert Brown, who first described the odd motion of pollen molecules suspended in water but could not explain it. In 1905, no less a figure than Albert Einstein, in his *annus mirabilis*, theorized that Brownian motion could be explained by the random collision of particles in water molecules, thus providing the first experimental evidence of the existence of atoms.

But Bachelier used Brownian motion to attempt to model financial stock prices a few years before Einstein explained its physics. Since then, the Nobel laureates Robert Merton, Fischer Black, and Myron Scholes independently arrived at the famous Black-Scholes-Merton (BSM) model, which provides a quasi-analytical solution to the value of a European call option on an asset whose spot price follows Brownian motion.[4]

More precisely, BSM assumes that spot price S_t follows a stochastic geometric Brownian (also known as log-normal) motion:

$$d\left(\log\left(S_t\right)\right) = \mu dt + \sigma dW_t \text{ or } dS_t = \mu S_t dt + \sigma S_t dW_t,$$

where $dW_t \sim N\left(0, dt\right)$.

The first term, μdt, characterizes the constant percentage drift or trend term that aims to model deterministic trends. The second term, σdW_t, characterizes the stochastic component, which captures random or unpredictable events. Here, W_t is a Wiener process, the continuous-time limit of infinitesimally small, normally distributed random walk steps. It is named in honor of the American mathematician Norbert Wiener for his mathematical contributions to the study of Brownian motion. The Wiener process is what gives the asset price its random component. Appendix 4.1 provides a primer on some basic stochastic calculus and a simplified proof of the BSM formula.

3. L. Bachelier, "Théorie de la speculation," *Annales Scientifiques de l'École Normale Supérieure* 3, no.17 (1900): 21–86.
4. Fischer Black and Myron Scholes, "The Pricing of Options and Corporate Liabilities," *Journal of Political Economy* 81, no. 3 (1973): 637–654 (doi:10.1086/26006); Robert C. Merton, "Theory of Rational Option Pricing," *Bell Journal of Economics and Management Science* 4, no. 1 (1973): 141–183 (doi:10.2307/3003143).

Since the payoff of a derivative can be replicated by a portfolio with a mix of the underlying stock and a bond at various positions, the price of the derivative can be found indirectly through the price of a replicating portfolio. Black, Scholes, and Merton demonstrated that the price of the option must satisfy a partial differential equation that eventually collapses to mimic the equation for heat from classical physics.

Then, for a European call option with expiry T and strike price K, the price of the option at time t, with the price of underlying asset S, is as follows:

$$V_{call}(S,t) = \Phi\left[\frac{\left(\ln\left(\frac{S(t)}{K}\right) + \left(r + \left(\frac{\sigma^2}{2}\right)\right)(T-t)\right)}{\sigma\sqrt{T-t}}\right].S(t)$$
$$-\Phi\left[\frac{\left(\ln\left(\frac{S(t)}{K}\right) + \left(r - \left(\frac{\sigma^2}{2}\right)\right)(T-t)\right)}{\sigma\sqrt{T-t}}\right].Ke^{-r(T-t)}$$

where

$\Phi(.)$ is the cumulative distribution of the standard normal distribution,
$(T-t)$ is the time to maturity,
$S(t)$ is the price of the underlying asset at time t,
K is the strike price,
r is the risk-free rate, and
σ is the volatility of returns of the underlying asset.

Once the European call option price has been valued, it is possible to find the value of a European put option by utilizing the put-call parity relationship. Graphically, this formula can be presented in three-dimensional space, reflecting the relationship between the price of the call option, V_{call}, the price of the underlying asset at time t, S_t, and the time to maturity, t (see figure 4.8). Close inspection of figure 4.8 shows that at maturity, the price of an option is exactly the same as the payoff profile (dotted line) shown in figure 4.7a. As we move further away from maturity, the price of an option has a one-to-one relationship with the price of the underlying asset. The dotted line reflects the price of the option as it approaches maturity. At this stage the price of the option depends on whether it is in the money or out of the money. If it is deep in the money, the price of the option converges to $S_t - PV(K)$

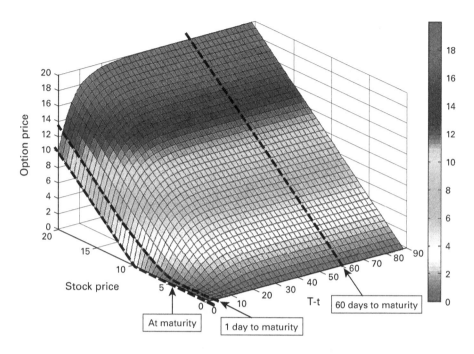

Figure 4.8
Price of a European option with strike price = $10, $T - t$ days to maturity, and underlying
security price S.
Source: Author's calculations.

to reflect the time value of money. The price converges to zero as the
price of the underlying asset moves out of the money. As the price of
the underlying asset falls into a range that is sufficiently close to the
strike price K, the price of the option is still positive and its valuation
is significantly affected by the implied volatility of the stock. This is
because the higher the volatility, the better chance the option has of
moving back into the money. Appendix 4.1 covers the Black-Scholes-
Merton model in more detail.

Beyond Call Options: Exotic Derivatives
From the basic building blocks of options pricing, financial practitioners have created an exotic menagerie of more complicated derivatives.
Some of these include bull spreads, bear spreads, butterflies, straddles,
and strangles. Much of Wall Street is home to a whole cottage industry
of these derivatives, while business schools produce academic research

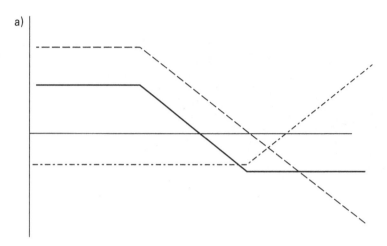

Figure 4.9a
Complex derivatives: bull spread position.

studying pricing behavior and the discrepancies from arbitrage-free markets of complex derivatives.

Let's discuss a few of these. The bull spread hedging strategy allows an investor to express a view that the price of the underlying asset will rise, but not too much. By buying a call option at price K and shorting a call option at a price higher than K, say, $K + e$, the investor exposes himself to gains only if the stock price at maturity falls within the range of K and $K + e$ (figure 4.9a). The investor effectively earns a premium by forgoing his earnings should the price of the underlying asset move above $K + e$. The idea here is, why pay for additional exposure when you believe that the price of the asset will not rise above $K + e$? The same intuition applies for the bear spread hedging strategy, but in a reverse scenario where one expects the price to fall, but not below the value of $K - e$. (figure 4.9b).

When compared to the bull and bear spread hedging strategy, the butterfly spread strategy is even more aggressive in that it only allows the investor to earn profits only if the price of the asset falls between the range of $K - e$ and $K + e$. Specifically, his profits will be maximized if the price of the underlying asset happens to be exactly equal to K at the point of maturity (figure 4.10). Although a positive payoff is less likely in this scenario, one should note that in the construction of a butterfly spread, the amount of premium earned by shorting the call option offsets most of the premium paid to buying the call option,

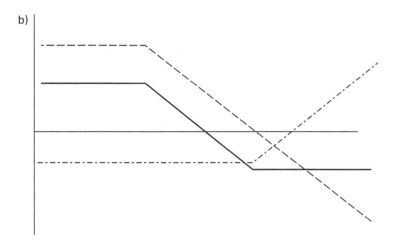

Figure 4.9b
Complex derivatives: bear spread position.

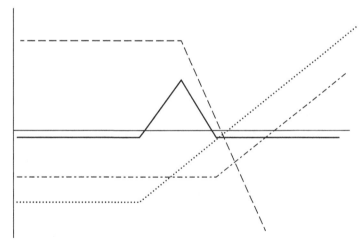

Figure 4.10
Complex derivatives: butterfly spread position.

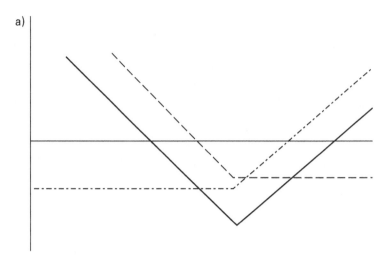

Figure 4.11a
Complex derivatives: straddle spread position.

rendering the butterfly spread little downside risk. A risk-loving investor would not mind exposing himself to a small downside risk for a
handsome gain should his prediction turn out to be true.

In contrast to the bull and bear spread hedging strategy, the straddle
and strangle spread strategies allow an investor to express a view that
the price of the asset will either increase or decrease sharply (figures
4.11a and b). The straddle and strangle spreads punish the investor
heavily should prices fail to move in any direction. Although the strangle spread minimizes the losses in the event of insufficient price movement, the investor faces a trade-off in that he will gain only if the price
of the underlying asset moves sufficiently far away from the strike
prices of the long call and long put positions. A straddle spread position would give the investor a higher probability of positive gains as
the strike prices of the long call and long put positions are much closer
to each other.

Conclusion

Commodity derivatives are not new, but it has taken a while for academics and practitioners to have a firm understanding of its usefulness
as well as the risks associated with employing them. Far from the
idyllic textbook world, the world of derivatives is still evolving through

b)

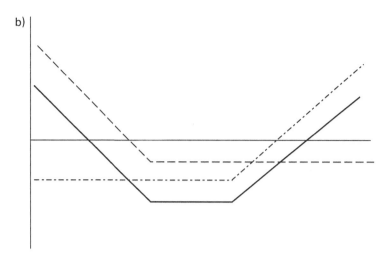

Figure 4.11b
Complex derivatives: strangle spread.

financial innovation and regulation—a pertinent issue in recent times given the increased regulatory scrutiny following the worldwide recession of 2008–2009. One useful application of option theory is in the world of investment valuation, better known as "real optionality." This theme is the topic of the next chapter.

Appendix 4.1 Primer on Ito Calculus, the Black-Scholes-Merton Model, and Greeks

Some Definitions

A *normal* distribution (also known as a standard or a Gaussian distribution in honor of German mathematician Carl Friedrich Gauss, 1777–1855) is a probability distribution for a random variable $X \sim N(\mu, \sigma^2)$ with probability density function:

$$f(x) = \frac{1}{\sigma\sqrt{2\pi}} e^{-\frac{(x-\mu)^2}{2\sigma^2}}.$$

The mean of the distribution is given by $E(X) = \mu$ and the variance is given by $E\left((X - \mu)^2\right) = \sigma^2$.

The normal distribution is ubiquitous in the natural and social sciences because of the *central limit theorem*, which loosely states that the sample averages of independent draws of any well-behaved random variable with finite mean and variance converges in distribution to a normal distribution with the same mean and variance linearly declining in the number of draws.

Central Limit Theorem
Let $X_1, X_2, \ldots, X_n$ be independent and identical draws from the any single distribution X with finite mean μ and variance σ^2.

Then the sample average $S_n = \dfrac{1}{n} \sum_{i=1}^{n} X_i$ converges in distribution to a normal distribution:

$$S_n \sim N\left(\mu, \frac{\sigma^2}{n}\right) \text{ as } n \to \infty.$$

The fact that the point estimate of the sample average converges to the probabilistic mean is known as the *law of large numbers*.

The ubiquity of normal distributions as a result of the central limit theorem should not blind us to the fact that it does not always apply. For example, certain extremely fat-tailed distributions in natural disasters and financial assets may feature parameterized power-law distributions with tail indices less than two—that is, the second moment does not exist. Then the central limit theorem breaks down.

Brownian Motion
A standard Brownian motion (also called a Wiener process, in honor of the American mathematician Norbert Wiener, 1894–1964) is a stochastic random variable $Z(t)$ such that:

- $Z(t)$ is an almost surely (i.e., with probability 1) everywhere a continuous function of t,
- $Z(0) = 0$, and
- $Z(t)$ has independent increments, with $Z(t) - Z(s) \sim N(0, t-s)$ for all $0 \leq s \leq t$, where $N(.,.)$ denotes the normal distribution.

Some history: Brownian motion is so named in honor of Robert Brown (1773–1858), a Scottish botanist who observed inexplicable "jittery" motions of a grain of pollen supposedly resting untouched in water.

Similar phenomena had been observed before, perhaps most remarkably by the Roman poet Lucretius (99–55 BC), who postulated the theory of atoms based on the motion of dust particles in air.

The French mathematician Louis Bachelier (1870–1946) proposed for his 1900 Ph.D. thesis under the French mathematician Henri Poincaré (1854–1912) to use a stochastic Brownian motion to describe the behavior of stock prices, which is now widely used. Perhaps because studying stock prices was not in fashion at the time, this contribution was not fully recognized at the time, and Bachelier's subsequent career was relatively undistinguished.

Albert Einstein (1879–1955) brought the matter of Brownian motion to the attention of his fellow physicists in a 1905 paper, "On the Motion of Small Particles Suspended in a Stationary Liquid, As Required by the Molecular Kinetic Theory of Heat." Einstein postulated a full theory of Brownian motion based on randomized collisions of atoms, thus forming an indirect but empirically testable theory based on the atomistic theory of matter, which was widely suspected but not proven, owing to the limitations on microscopes of the time. This was subsequently proven by French physicist Jean Perrin (1870–1942) in 1926. Brownian motion forms one of Einstein's four great 1905 *annus mirabilis* contributions, along with the photoelectric effect, special relativity, and mass-energy equivalence.

Ito's Calculus and Ito's Lemma

A stochastic process or Ito process (named in honor of the Japanese mathematician Ito Kiyoshi, 1915–2008) is a random variable that accumulates from the addition of multiple infinitesimal Brownian motions. It consists of a deterministic trend component and a stochastic component:

$$X(t) = X(0) + \int_0^t \mu(s)ds + \int_0^t \sigma(s)dZ(s),$$

and is often rewritten in differential form as

$$dX(t) = \mu(t)dt + \sigma(t)dZ(t),$$

where $\mu(t)$ and $\sigma(t)$ are continuous measurable functions and $dZ(t)$ is a Brownian motion $\sim N(0, dt)$.

Then, for any twice differentiable function $f(x, t)$, Ito's lemma states that:

$$df(X(t),t) = \left[\frac{\partial f}{\partial t}(X(t),t) + \mu(t)\frac{\partial f}{\partial x}(X(t),t) + \frac{\sigma(t)^2}{2}\frac{\partial^2 f}{\partial x^2}(X(t),t)\right]dt$$
$$+ \sigma(t)\frac{\partial f}{\partial x}(X(t),t)dZ(t).$$

Informal "Proof":
Basically, the rule of thumb to remember is that $dZ(t)$ is of order $\sqrt{dt}$.

Expand the twice differentiable $df(X(t),t)$ via its Taylor expansion around $t + dt$:

$$df = f(X + dX, t + dt) - f(X,t),$$

$$= \frac{\partial f}{\partial t}dt + \frac{\partial f}{\partial x}dX + \frac{1}{2}\frac{\partial^2 f}{\partial x^2}dX^2 + \ldots$$

Substituting in our stochastic process, we get:

$$= \frac{\partial f}{\partial t}dt + \frac{\partial f}{\partial x}[\mu dt + \sigma dZ] + \frac{1}{2}\frac{\partial^2 f}{\partial x^2}[\mu^2 dt^2 + 2\mu\sigma dtdZ + \sigma^2 dZ^2] + \ldots$$

As $dt \to 0$, all terms of order higher than dt drop out, including terms of order dt^2 and $dtdZ$.

But dZ^2 is of order dt, since it is the second moment of the infinitesimal Brownian motion with variance dt. Collecting terms, we get:

$$df = \left[\frac{\partial f}{\partial t} + \mu\frac{\partial f}{\partial x} + \frac{\sigma^2}{2}\frac{\partial^2 f}{\partial x^2}\right]dt + \sigma\frac{\partial f}{\partial x}dZ.$$

Black-Scholes-Merton Model
The American mathematician Fischer Black (1938–1995) and the Canadian economist Myron Scholes (1941–), working together, and the American economist Robert C. Merton (1944–), working independently, derived a formula for pricing European call options. They had different approaches, Black and Scholes using the intuition of a replicating portfolio, Merton using a partial differential equation argument. There is an alternative way that recognizes the value of the derivative is equal to the expected payoff, that is, it is a martingale, under a risk-neutral probability density.

The BSM model assumes that the underlying stock asset S follows a *geometric Brownian motion*, also known as a *log-normal* distribution:

$$dS = \mu S dt + \sigma S dZ.$$

Then consider the value of a European call option V with strike price K and expiration at $t = T$. The payoff at expiration would be:

$$V(S(T), T) = \max(S(T) - K, 0).$$

What is the value $V(S(t), t)$?

Consider an arbitrageur who decides to borrow sufficient money to construct a portfolio containing one long call option, having partially financed this by selling short Δ shares of the underlying stock. The portfolio would be worth:

$$\Pi = V - \Delta S$$

By using Ito's Lemma, we can derive:

$$d\Pi = dV - \Delta dS,$$

$$= \left[\frac{\partial V}{\partial t} + \mu S \frac{\partial V}{\partial S} + \frac{\sigma^2}{2} S^2 \frac{\partial^2 V}{\partial S^2} \right] dt + \sigma S \frac{\partial f}{\partial S} dZ - \Delta \mu S dt - \Delta \sigma S dZ,$$

$$= \left[\frac{\partial V}{\partial t} + \mu S \frac{\partial V}{\partial S} + \frac{\sigma^2}{2} S^2 \frac{\partial^2 V}{\partial S^2} - \Delta \mu S \right] dt + \left[\sigma S \frac{\partial f}{\partial S} - \Delta \sigma S \right] dZ.$$

Suppose we set $\Delta = \dfrac{\partial V}{\partial S}$. Then the stochastic term vanishes and the portfolio becomes riskless! To prevent risk-neutral arbitrage, this portfolio should earn the risk-free rate r:

$$d\Pi = r\Pi dt,$$

$$\left[\frac{\partial V}{\partial t} + \frac{\sigma^2}{2} S^2 \frac{\partial^2 V}{\partial S^2} \right] dt = r \left[V - S \frac{\partial V}{\partial S} \right] dt.$$

Rearranging, we derive the Black-Scholes-Merton partial differential equation:

$$rV = \frac{\partial V}{\partial t} + rS \frac{\partial V}{\partial S} + \frac{\sigma^2}{2} S^2 \frac{\partial^2 V}{\partial S^2}.$$

Merton demonstrated how, with a change of variables, this can be rewritten into a diffusion equation, the one-dimension version being known as the heat equation.

Consider the change of variables as follows:

$$\tau = \frac{\sigma^2}{2}(T - t), \quad x = \ln\left(\frac{S}{K}\right), \quad u = e^{ax + b\tau} \frac{V}{K},$$

where

$$a = 1 - \frac{k}{2}, b = -\frac{1}{4}(k+1)^2, \text{ and } k = \frac{2r}{\sigma^2}.$$

One can show after substitution and simplifying that the original PDE becomes:

$$\frac{\partial u}{\partial \tau} = \frac{\partial^2 u}{\partial x^2},$$

which is the one-dimensional version of the heat equation:

$$\frac{\partial u}{\partial t} = \alpha \Delta^2 u.$$

The one-dimension problem is known to have the following solution:

$$u(x,t) = u(x,0) * \Phi(x,t),$$

where $\Phi(x,t) = \dfrac{1}{\sqrt{4\pi\alpha t}} e^{-\frac{x^2}{4\alpha t}}$ and $*$ is the convolution operator:

$$(f*g)(x) = \int_{-\infty}^{\infty} f(x-y) g(y) dy.$$

Intuitively, the solution to the BSM PDE looks like a "heat diffusion" from the final quasi-linear payoff function at expiration "leaking" backward in time at a rate proportional to half the variance.

The Financial "Greeks"
Delta measures the rate of change of the option value with respect to the underlying asset:

$$\Delta = \frac{\partial V}{\partial S}.$$

Gamma measures the second-order rate of change of delta with respect to the underlying asset:

$$\Gamma = \frac{\partial \Delta}{\partial S} = \frac{\partial^2 V}{\partial S^2}.$$

Vega measures the rate of change of the option value with respect to the volatility of the underlying asset:

$$V = \frac{\partial V}{\partial \sigma}.$$

Theta measures the rate of change of the option value with respect to the passage of time to expiration, the time decay:

$$\Theta = -\frac{\partial V}{\partial \tau}.$$

Rho measures the rate of change of the option value with respect to the interest rate:

$$\rho = \frac{\partial V}{\partial r}.$$

5 Economics and Financial Activities behind Derivatives

We begin this chapter with a short story. Barrick Gold, one of the largest gold mining companies in the world, used to be famous for hedging nearly all of its gold production. This strategy proved popular with shareholders as long as its hedging strategy made money, and its stock price tended to be higher relative to that of its peers in large part because of its successful hedging exploits. Yet things changed dramatically in 2000, when gold prices rose, the futures curve moved into backwardation, and Barrick began losing money on its hedge book. Finally, with shareholders fed up, Barrick dramatically changed its approach to hedging and announced a 180-degree shift: it would stop hedging entirely. Which was the right strategy for Barrick?

Barrick's flip-flop is symptomatic of a broader debate among companies and investors as to the rationale for and methods of using financial markets and derivatives in the commodities space. Should companies hedge to safeguard against changing prices? Should they do it to reap a direct profit by trading on superior information? Or should they simply avoid the practice altogether? What about speculators and investors who don't have other revenue streams to hedge? Are they mere money-grubbers, profiting off the backs of others? Do they play a positive role in markets? Or should they be strictly regulated or even banned from the markets?

This chapter attempts to untangle this debate and shed some light on the potential value of both hedging and speculating when these activities are done properly. We begin with a discussion of hedging—why it should be done and when it can succeed—then continue with an overview of speculation and how, under certain circumstances, it can be socially beneficial. The chapter concludes with a brief discussion of how the aforementioned activities can affect the working of commodity markets.

Hedging Commodity Risk: Motivations and Methods

Why would companies want to hedge commodity risk? According to standard corporate finance theory, the famous Modigliani-Miller theorem states that hedging should add no value to a company at all! (We won't go into a review of Modigliani-Miller theorem; readers unfamiliar with it should find any corporate finance textbook a good refresher.) The theorem states that under perfect capital market conditions without taxes, bankruptcy costs, or asymmetric information, purely financial transactions should not affect the ultimate value of the firm. So why would a firm spend time, money, and resources on hedging if it does not add any value to the company?

The Modigliani-Miller theorem was never meant to be taken literally. Rather, it serves as a useful guide to the reasons why firms should hedge, namely, when bankruptcy costs, taxes, or asymmetric information matter or when capital markets are imperfect:

- **Tax benefits**: As we have seen, commodity prices can be very volatile, and it can be tax-efficient for a firm to smooth its income rather than pay high taxes on windfalls.
- **Avoiding bankruptcy costs**: Bankruptcy and other forms of financial distress impose large direct and indirect costs on a firm, ranging from the cost of hiring the necessary legal and accounting expertise for a bankruptcy process to weakened credit quality and the loss of human capital. Hedging commodity price risk can help avoid such bankruptcy costs.
- **Ensuring cash flow for optimal investment**: This point is perhaps the most important reason why firms should hedge and is worth going into in more detail.

In an ideal world, in which capital markets are perfect, all economic value-adding projects should be properly capitalized. But the world is not perfect, and there are many projects for which firms may have trouble raising sufficient capital. Indeed, most private sector projects are done not by raising capital directly for the project (as in project finance) but based on some host company's balance sheet. Hence, ensuring that a company has sufficient internal cash flow to cover all of its optimal investment needs is critical; this is where hedging comes in.

Figure 5.1 illustrates how hedging can help match a company's investment needs to its internal supply of capital. We can take as an

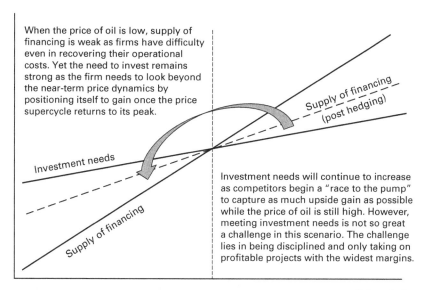

When the price of oil is low, supply of financing is weak as firms have difficulty even in recovering their operational costs. Yet the need to invest remains strong as the firm needs to look beyond the near-term price dynamics by positioning itself to gain once the price supercycle returns to its peak.

Investment needs

Supply of financing (post hedging)

Supply of financing

Investment needs will continue to increase as competitors begin a "race to the pump" to capture as much upside gain as possible while the price of oil is still high. However, meeting investment needs is not so great a challenge in this scenario. The challenge lies in being disciplined and only taking on profitable projects with the widest margins.

Price of oil

Figure 5.1
A stylized graph of a company's supply of financing versus investment needs.

example a prototypical upstream oil producer. Naturally, its cash flow revenue (the steeply sloped line in figure 5.1) goes up as the price of oil (on the horizontal axis) goes up. Its investment needs may also go up as the price of oil goes up, since more projects become economical at higher oil prices. But it probably does not go up as steeply since oil prices are highly volatile and project life cycles can span decades or more. The company wants to make sure that a project stays economically sound through future troughs in the commodity supercycle, even though the price of oil is high now and the company is flush with cash. Conversely, when the price of oil is low, there may be projects the company would like to invest in now that the longer-term outlook for oil is brighter.

This creates a clear disconnect between the company's supply of financing and its investments needs, with the company having more cash than needed for its internal investments when the price of oil is high and not enough cash to finance all its desired projects when the price of oil is low. Hedging thus allows a firm to transfer income from a "high-price" state to a "low-price" state, reducing the mismatch between investment needs and supply of funds.

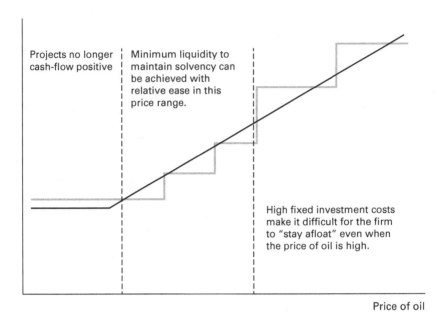

Figure 5.2
A more realistic graph of a company's supply of financing versus investment needs.

The company might have sold its oil production forward when futures prices were relatively high, ensuring that sufficient cash flow would be available when times were low. Or it might have bought put options and sold call options to directly offload price upside risk and gain low-price protection. But in short, by hedging, the company has lessened the slope of its cash flow from the solid line to the dotted line, bringing its internal demand for and supply of capital into closer alignment.

Of course, figure 5.1 is highly stylized, and investment demand schedules are not as straightforward or as simple as the upward-sloping line might suggest. Figure 5.2 is slightly more realistic, with a stepwise function for investment capital demand that jumps as projects become economical in a lumpy fashion because of initial fixed costs. Perhaps when commodity prices are extremely low, there is a flat floor of investment demand from operating expenses to simply ensure that the company remains solvent and avoids bankruptcy.

Every company faces a unique investment landscape. But the CFO of every resource-exposed company should have a firm grasp of its internal demand and supply curves for capital and should view the use of hedging and financial derivatives as a powerful tool to bring those into neat alignment for optimal value creation for the firm.

Sadly, it appears that this rationale is lost on many companies and their shareholders. Recall our example of Barrick Gold, whose irate shareholders forced the company to cease hedging entirely after a long history of money-losing hedge trades. Why wasn't this a rational move? After all, the skeptics might say, the hedge books were losing money. But that's not the point.

Let's take the example of the airline business. Suppose a fictitious airline, call it Alpha Airlines, fearful that a spike in jet fuel prices might limit its ability to make capital investments in a desired fleet upgrade, decides to hedge its commodity price risk by purchasing $100 million worth of call options on oil. But a competitor—say, Beta—does not.

Let's see what happens if jet fuel prices do *not* go up. Then Alpha has "lost" $100 million by purchasing a call option that expires out of the money. Shareholders demand to know why Alpha Airlines has hedge book losses on its balance sheet compared to its rival Beta. Alpha's stock prices underperform relative to Beta's, its management gets punished for engaging in silly money-losing financial shenanigans, and a new, chastened leadership announces it will no longer hedge—which is what actually happened to Barrick Gold.

This is rather unfair and nonsensical. The investors ignored what would have happened had jet fuel prices increased. Then Alpha's hedge book would have risen in value by, say, $200 million, and its management would probably have been lionized for its brilliant foresight in protecting against oil price spikes that its rivals failed to consider.

But this is still beside the point, as the hedging strategy was never about directly making money on the book, it was about aligning the company's capital supply with its optimal investment needs. The $200 million gain was to cover the additional expenses resulting from higher jet fuel costs in the normal operation of Alpha's fleet and still have money left over to meet any additional capital requirements. Likewise, a $100 million loss if oil prices fell would have been made up for by lower fuel bills and other expenses *since the oil prices fell, and that is a good thing for airlines*. Whether the book "made" or "lost" money is meaningless.

Here we may draw an analogy with an insurance contract against a natural disaster. This is also a form of hedging, in this case against a loss of income arising from an admittedly unlikely occurrence, such as a fire or a car accident. When the disaster does *not* occur, the holder of the insurance contract "loses" by having paid money to protect against an outcome that didn't happen. (This is how insurance companies make money, after all.) Yet in such cases, individuals and investors do not seem too unduly disposed to punish and ridicule someone for buying an insurance contract that subsequently "loses" money. (Can you imagine the absurdity of being angry at someone for buying accident insurance and being upset because the accident didn't happen?)

Despite a similar logic being applicable to commodity risk hedging, agents and investors are predisposed to be suspicious of hedging, and financial losses on accounting books due to hedging are castigated as a sign of poor management. This double standard between buying insurance and hedging is an unfortunate behavioral anomaly. Shareholders are irrationally averse to hedging book losses relative to an irrational benchmark, such as the no-hedging activity of a competitor, regardless of reality and the hedging needs of the firm.

Systematically abused, this behavioral anomaly can have significant macroscopic consequences. If companies are forced to always make money on their hedge book regardless of their internal cash flow needs, then they are acting like speculators, not hedgers! And indeed, many companies, under the guise of being commercial hedgers, speculate plenty. We discuss the rationale for speculation in the next section, but it is important to realize that the seemingly clear theoretical line between hedgers and speculators is often blurred in reality. Many companies with physical exposure to commodities speculate intensively as another component of their business strategy. Later, we also discuss long-term institutional investors in commodities, who in many ways are akin to hedgers, despite their purely financial interests.

By denying companies the ability to make proper investments when commodity prices are low and only allowing investments when prices are high, this behavioral anomaly distorts markets and exacerbates the commodity supercycle. If massive investments in capital-intensive projects can occur only when prices are high and companies are cash-rich, this will sow the seeds for a price crash as overcapacity is built up. Likewise, when prices are low and companies are not sufficiently investing in projects to come online in the future, there will be insufficient supply in a few years when demand comes back, causing prices to soar. The economic dislocation from this commodity supercycle (not to mention the often dire political consequences) can and should be properly tempered by company hedging to smooth both corporate income streams and investment cycles.

We should recognize one final reason why companies may be the best agents to hedge, and not individual investors. That reason has to do with the Modigliani-Miller theorem on capital structure. The rationale behind the proof of the theorem was that if any purely financial transactions or capital restructuring could add value to the company, then private investors could arbitrage that value creation by replicating the hedging strategy themselves.

This logic has led some academics and corporate strategists to argue that companies still should not hedge because individual investors are better placed to hedge commodity price risk themselves rather than having companies do it. Indeed, some argue that investors may want to become shareholders in certain resource-exposed firms (e.g., Exxon-Mobil) precisely because those companies do not hedge, and therefore shareholders can gain a full, undiluted exposure to commodity risk through owning shares in them.

That argument, however, is misguided. First, small investors face much steeper transaction costs as sophisticated derivative trading requires significant investment in both the technology and the talent to conduct it properly. Only firms have the size and scale to minimize transaction costs to hedge properly, not to mention having access to high-quality internal intelligence about the state of the markets (this can also make them superior speculators).

If investors want commodity price exposure, there are now many instruments, such as exchange-traded funds (ETFs) and master limited partnerships (MLPs), that can give retail investors direct access to commodity risk and risk premia. It is absurd to require that companies cease hedging and risk potential damage to their own value just so that shareholders can get undiluted commodity exposure.

A company like ExxonMobil, for example, is famous for not hedging at all, instead relying entirely on its "fortress" balance sheet to ride out commodity price cycles and ensure sufficient capital to maintain optimal investment in projects. ExxonMobil boasts world-class engineers and geologists and often commands a share price premium relative to peers. But relying solely on a cash cushion is a very expensive way to hedge, as it requires the company to be holding sufficient cash in *all* contingencies, not just when it needs it for sufficient investment. For all of Exxon's laudable strengths, it behooves economists and analysts to ask themselves whether that surplus cash sitting on Exxon's balance sheets might be put to more efficient use in shareholders' hands.

However, it is worth noting that other factors may come into play when a potential corporate hedger has market power (or has national sovereignty). If a firm has market power, then hedging may be less relevant since the firm has the power to modify prices anyway. There may still be a disconnect between its internal supply of and needs for capital, but there's another problem. Any counterparty to the hedging transaction would be unwilling to take the other side. After all, if the counterparty to whom a trader is, for example, selling a call option has the power to ensure spot prices always hit above the strike price at the delivery date, why would the trader ever agree to the transaction in the first place? The counterparty can always manipulate prices to ensure that the trader would *always* lose money.

Similarly, if the counterparty is a state-owned enterprise, how can the trader have the confidence to enforce the contract if it is a money-losing proposition to the other side? A state-owned enterprise, beyond a court's legal jurisdiction, may simply renege on its fiduciary obligations and hide behind its sovereign immunity. These issues can weaken the depth of financial markets for hedging activity, especially in markets such as oil, where sovereign state-owned enterprises are often the natural hedgers, with large exposure to commodity resources. (State-owned enterprises in the commodity sector are discussed in chapter 9.)

Speculation and the Economic Calculation Problem

The other class of market participants consists of speculators. It is a widely held view that speculators are little better than gamblers making mindless bets on the "market price casino" or, even worse, deliberately manipulating the market to extract profits at the expense of innocent consumers and producers. While there certainly are such malicious actors in the markets, it is unfair to condemn all speculation in such a blanket fashion.

The American journalist Charles Conant (1861–1915) gave one of the earliest cogent defenses of speculation in a 1901 article titled "The Uses of Speculation." Conant argued that market prices summarized for free public use useful information held by market participants about the "true value" of a good. This price signal helped producers and consumers in their complex planning decisions and ultimately ensured a more efficient allocation of resources. Speculators helped this price discovery. All the sophisticated research and expensive investigations into demand and supply conditions done by speculators in support of their trading decisions would be expressed in publicly visible prices *through those very same speculative trades*. If speculators felt the price of a commodity was too low or too high and not properly representative of the true state of supply and demand, they would attempt to arbitrage the difference. But in doing so, they would force the price back toward the "true" equilibrium, and the entire economy would enjoy the fruits of the speculators' labor.

The debate over the role of prices in economic decision making highlighted by Conant is an antecedent of the famous debate in economics known as the *economic calculation problem*. In the 1930s, when the capitalist world was in the throes of the Great Depression, the Soviet Union's command-and-control system of ambitious Five-Year Plans was seemingly moving ahead by leaps and bounds. This stirred a profound existential debate over the nature of capitalism itself: was the capitalist system based on market principles sustainable, or was it doomed to be outperformed by command economies led by benevolent and far-seeing planners?

The economists Ludwig von Mises and Friedrich Hayek constructed a powerful defense of capitalism by formulating the economic calculation problem. For all of the vaunted wisdom and benevolence of a central planner, von Mises argued, no single person or entity, no matter how intelligent and well resourced, could possibly track all the information and do all the complex calculations necessary to properly allocate resources efficiently in a modern economy. The calculation problem is simply too hard for a central planner (and the Soviet Union had tried, building some of the most advanced supercomputers of the day for use by their economic planners at Gosplan). Hayek went further, warning of the political tyranny that would result on the "road to serfdom" from ceding to the state control of all economic decision making. By contrast, a market economy decentralizes economic decision making into thousands of subdecisions made by individual consumers and firms (somewhat analogous to distributed computing), all connected through the mechanism of market prices. It is essential that these prices be able to freely float and react to private decision making and trading activity. Adam Smith's famous invisible hand would then ensure that these subdecisions would aggregate toward a socially optimal outcome, and the economic calculation problem would be solved.

But for the market to properly allocate resources, market prices need to be representative of the true value of products. And for markets to be able to successfully determine the appropriate level of prices, market participants, including speculators, need good information about the true state of the market. Economists might simply shrug and say any mispricing from the true equilibrium would cause supply and demand mismatches that would show up in growing or shrinking storage levels (indeed, the Nobel laureate Paul Krugman made such an argument in *New York Times* op-eds when oil prices were approaching record highs in 2007). But in many commodity markets, where information about demand, supply, and storage is often incomplete or not trustworthy, it can be very hard for markets to function effectively. We will return to this point shortly.

In such poor market conditions, traders may be tempted to simply copy the behavior of others, hoping that the crowd knows something they don't. But the herd phenomena caused by such copycat behavior can inject excess volatility into the market. Speculators may leap in, betting less on any superior understanding of commodity market fundamentals than on how crowd psychology works. At its worst, herd behavior can cause irrational frenzies and precipitate dramatic market distortions away from true equilibrium value, in much the same way that lemmings are led to apocryphally leap off cliffs to their doom. Thus financial bubbles born.

Some of the ingredients of effective financial regulation to ensure market efficiency in commodity markets are discussed in chapter 10, but it is worth repeating that such malignant market distortions should not be misapprehended and used to justify a blanket condemnation of markets or speculation.

In Conant's words, "The remedy for the misuse of a delicate and useful machine is not to smash the machine, but to do all that is possible to restrict it to its legitimate use."

A Simple Model of Price Discovery

To wrap up this chapter, we consider a simple model for price discovery and inventory building. This model was developed by Kenneth Medlock of Rice University's Baker Institute and serves as a useful framework for understanding the relationships among demand, supply, storage (or inventories), and financial activity. The model integrates the markets for resource flows (e.g., immediate consumption and production), the accumulation and release of storage inventory stocks, and financial expectations.

Let's first concentrate on the flow side of the market. We assume immediate demand d_t is downward sloping in the current spot price p_t but is also affected by other exogenous factors x_t, such as income or seasonality. Meanwhile, the immediate flow supply of the commodity q_t depends not on current prices but instead on existing investment i_t and a decaying factor on previous flow production γq_{t-1}. This might be interpreted as production from oil fields with a constant decline rate γ. In turn, investment i_t depends not on current prices but on expectations of future prices, $E_t(p_{t+1})$, minus some cost factor, c_{t+1}.

Formula 5.3: Flow

Demand function:

$$d_t = b_0 - b_1 p_t + b_2 x_t.$$

Supply function:

$$q_t = i_t + \gamma q_{t-1} = \eta\left[E_t(p_{t+1}) - c_{t+1}\right] + \gamma q_{t-1},$$

$$i_t - new\ investment,$$

$$\gamma q_{t-1} - declining\ production,$$

Now let's turn to the market for commodity stocks or inventories. Demand for inventory is assumed to be a declining function of current spot prices but an increasing function of the current futures price for next period's delivery, F_t^{t+1}. This is motivated by the Working-Kaldor theory of storage seen previously, where storage operators are motivated to store more commodities the greater the degree of contango in the futures curve. Meanwhile, the supply for inventory stock is more straightforward: current supply equals previous supply plus whatever surplus was produced over what was consumed:

Formula 5.3: Stock/Inventory

Demand function:

$$D_t = a_0 - a_1 p_t + a_2 F_t^{t+1}.$$

Supply function:

$$I_t = I_{t-1} + q_t - d_t.$$

Some simple algebra equating the demand and supply curves for both stocks and flows brings us the market-clearing equilibrium price. We see that prices depend not just on current exogenous demand factors but also on futures prices, expectations of future spot prices, and last period's inventory levels and supply.

Formula 5.4: Market-Clearing Equilibrium

$$p_t = \frac{a_0 + b_0}{a_1 + b_1} + \frac{b_2}{a_1 + b_1} x_t - \frac{1}{a_1 + b_1}\left[\eta\left(E_t\left[p_{t+1}\right] - c_{t+1}\right) + \gamma q_{t-1}\right]$$

$$-\frac{1}{a_1 + b_1} I_{t-1} + \frac{a_2}{a_1 + b_1} F_t^{t+1}.$$

This last dependence shows a key characteristic of this simple model: it is *self-correcting*. If ever there is excess flow supply $q_t > d_t$ over demand, then inventory levels I_t start to swell by $\Delta I_t = q_t - d_t$, putting downward pressure on prices and downward pressure on spot prices, p_t^{mkt} (possibly overshooting long-term equilibrium levels). Lower spot prices depress flow supply, increase flow demand, lower future price expectations, and weaken investment, until flow markets equalize. At this point, market prices p_t^{mkt} approach the true equilibrium price, p_t^{true}. We see this graphically in figure 5.3.

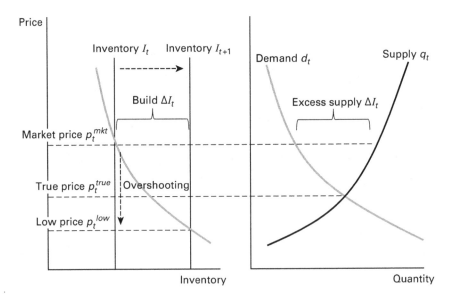

Figure 5.3
The market for commodity stocks and flows.

This self-correcting behavior by the mutual relationship between the spot market for flow commodities and the storage market for stock commodities has led some commentators to argue that some potential commodity market mispricings, such as the 2007 spike in oil prices, weren't mispricings at all since inventory levels were not growing. But reality is not always as neat as this nice picture of Adam Smith's invisible hand at work.

As we saw in previous chapters, the price elasticities of both supply and demand for commodities can be notoriously small. This means that in the flow market, the demand and supply curves are nearly vertical, meaning the ultimate inventory changes stemming from excess demand or supply can be very small. When coupled with high opacity, a lot of noise, and little transparency regarding the state of inventories in many parts of the world (for many commodity markets are fungible and globally integrated), small price elasticities create a fertile environment for financial bubbles and long-lived deviations of the market price away from true equilibrium prices, as shown in figure 5.4.

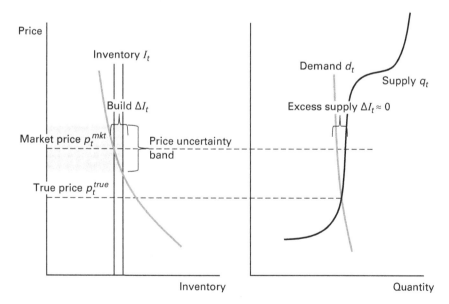

Figure 5.4
Stock and flow markets when markets are inelastic and opaque.

This opacity also tempts investors to follow the actions of others, creating herd behavior and exacerbating unnatural or excess volatility. This unnatural volatility can be difficult to distinguish from natural volatility but can cause massive real damage to economies and societies. Again, this shouldn't prompt us to denounce financial markets and speculators wholesale. But it does mean we must think carefully about how the market should be regulated. We address this topic in chapter 10, on regulation.

Module III: Valuation and Portfolio Choice

This module takes up commodity investment decisions faced by resource companies and financial investors.

How should resource companies decide when and which commodity projects should be invested in? How should such projects be valued?

And in turn, how should long-term financial investors and speculators approach commodities? Can investing in commodities serve as a good source of portfolio protection against inflation? As a source of alpha outperformance?

In chapter 6 we discuss the new theory of investment, which goes beyond classic net present value methodologies, and the sources of economic value unlocked by taking advantage of real optionality in projects.

In chapter 7 we discuss the relationship between commodity prices and inflation, and how commodities can serve as a hedge against unexpected inflation shocks in a long-term financial portfolio.

Finally, in chapter 8 we explore the alpha portfolio outperformance gained from reaping the risk premia inherent in commodity calendar spreads.

6   Real Optionality and Valuation

The standard treatment of the theory of investment often begins with discounted cash flows and net present value (NPV). If a project has a positive NPV, it is generating cash flow in excess of the interest rate (or the rate of return on capital invested passively in a bank), and investing in the project is economically valuable. Alternatively, investors can calculate a project's internal rate of return (IRR), the discount rate necessary to make a project's NPV zero, and compare that threshold to the investor's required rate of return on capital controlled for the amount of riskiness of the project.

In special cases in which project investments are perfectly reversible and there is perfect information, the standard NPV/IRR approach can a usefully aid in determining whether or not to move forward with a resource project. But this is rarely the case in reality. Although robustness tests—such as stress testing the project economics under high, base, or low scenarios for prices, volumes, and costs—can help overcome some of the shortcomings of these traditional theories of investment, more sophisticated methods have emerged to capture the full value of many resource projects. These methods emerged from the study of financial options (discussed in the previous chapters) and formed the theoretical foundation for a modernized New Theory of Investment. This "real optionality" approach has wide applicability to the study of many resource projects.

A New Theory of Investment Valuation: Real Optionality

Following the development of the Black-Scholes-Merton formula for the valuation of European call options, Avinash Dixit of Princeton and Robert Pindyck of MIT developed a real optionality approach to investment decisions that applies when the investment is irreversible or costly to adjust and when information is imperfect.[1]

Dixit and Pindyck noticed that the payoff structures of many assets mimic the payoff structure of financial options. For example, capital investors have the ability but not the obligation to invest in an asset, which affords the investor flexibility over the exact timing of the investment, in much the same way that the owner of an American option has the flexibility to choose when to exercise it. Fundamentally, this freedom to adapt to changing economic circumstances and new information is itself valuable and can be measured.

There are many potential sources of real optionality in investment projects, and the following are just a few commonly seen examples:

• Abandonment optionality is analogous to a put option on the project value. Once a project fails to deliver positive NPV, the investor or operator has the option to it shut down and walk away entirely. This may be costly but is clearly less so than continuously subsidizing an unprofitable project. This is like having a put option that one can exercise when the value of the project drops below zero, the "strike price" of the project.

• Deferment optionality provides investors the flexibility to postpone a project, which is analogous to having an American call option on the project value. For example, an oil driller may decide to acquire subsurface land rights but not begin drilling immediately, instead waiting for more opportune circumstances before completing the well and allowing the hydrocarbon molecules to flow. This ability of the investor or operator to adopt a "wait and see" approach in making investment decisions is itself economically valuable.

• Reversible shutdown optionality provides project managers the flexibility to contract or shut down *temporarily* if the project is unprofitable. For example, a peak load natural gas–powered generator typically runs only during peak power demand periods, when the price of electricity exceeds the cost of gas input. In nonpeak periods, it shuts down temporarily rather than continue to run unprofitably. This reversible shutdown option is analogous to a continuous stream of European call options.

From these examples, it is apparent that real optionality is ubiquitous in the space of commodity projects. Some other energy investment

1. Avinash K. Dixit and Robert S. Pindyck, *Investment under Uncertainty* (Princeton, NJ: Princeton University Press, 1994).

projects that have a clear "real optionality" associated with them are described below.

• *Unconventional shale/tight oil and gas fields.* Relative to conventional production, tight/shale oil and gas producers face a more "just-in-time" manufacturing-style process. The nature of hydraulic fracturing implies a rapid turnaround between the phases of well drilling, fracking, completion, and final production, which can be as short as a year compared to the decades-long life spans of conventional projects. As such, investors in unconventional oil and gas fields have more flexibility to *time* their activity to opportune market conditions. Companies took advantage of real optionality in 2014 by leaving wells drilled but uncompleted (DUC), holding their powder dry and waiting for the inevitable pickup in oil prices. This timing of investment is disrupting traditional notions of what is a "breakeven" price for energy projects and changing the very structure of price elasticities for global oil supply curve.

• *Storage facilities.* A storage facility by itself does not generate value but, as covered in the discussion of resource supply in chapter 1, allows an operator to shift resource supply across time to take advantage of price differentials in the futures market. This makes a storage facility a quintessential "real option," unable to be assessed by standard NPV methods but generating significant value through its optionality to adapt to market dynamics.

• *A pipeline with reversible flow or convertibility.* A pipeline has significant optionality through its ability to be reversed, its capacity expanded through higher pressurization, or even its ability to be converted to carry something else (e.g., refined product rather than crude oil). Notably, in the United States, the fracking revolution has upended the traditional flow of crude oil from the Gulf of Mexico inland, with oil from North Dakota and Texas now moving southward out toward the Gulf of Mexico. This development has required a major shift in pipeline flows, with many pipelines being reversed or repurposed to accommodate the new supply-and-demand landscape.

• *A peaking power plant.* The economics of a gas-fired power plant were mentioned above. Unlike a nuclear or hydroelectric power plant providing baseload power generation, peaking power plants are designed to be turned on and off at virtually no cost. They are intended to supply power only during periods of peak demand by way of a real-time bidding process in a merit-order dispatch system.

(The economics of electricity markets are discussed in greater depth in a later chapter.)

And just like any financial option, real options hold non-negative economic value since, at worst, one need not exercise the option.[2] And when the value is positive, it can become quite a significant part of the overall value of the project and decisive in determining whether it is a worthy investment or not. Let's turn to some more concrete examples to see how real optionality valuation may work in practice.

A Simple Example

Let's begin with a very simple and stylized example. Consider a project to develop an oil field that would require an initial capital expenditure of $160 million and would produce one million barrels per year in perpetuity. Its yearly required operating expenditure is $10/bbl. We'll assume a constant discount rate of 10%.

Assume the oil market price is currently $30/bbl but there is uncertainty in the future price of oil. For simplicity, suppose there is a 50% probability that the price will rise to $40/bbl next year and stay there forever, and a 50% probability that the price will fall to $20/bbl and stay there forever. (So the expected future price of oil is still $30/bbl in perpetuity.)

The standard NPV analysis would discount an infinite stream of annual expected profits of $20 million (($(0.5*20+0.5*40) − $10/bbl) × 1 mb/yr = $10 million) every year at 10% against a one-time investment of $160 million. After some simple arithmetic, we see the NPV is $60 million. This is positive, so the classic NPV framework would give the project a green light.

But suppose the investor has the flexibility to wait one year to see what happens to the price of oil. There can be immense economic value in having the option of waiting a year to see what the price of oil turns out to be. Then, if the price of oil does drop to $20/bbl, the NPV of the project is −$50 million, while if the price of oil goes up to $40/bbl, the NPV is $170 million. There is a cost to having to wait one year (the time

2. Actually, this is not quite true. In certain game-theoretic situations where the environment responds endogenously to the player's actions, there may be economic gains in *eliminating* optionality. This was the logic behind the famous "Doomsday Machine" proposed by RAND strategist Herman Kahn (popularized in the Stanley Kubrick film), where the removal of human control over a Doomsday Device provided the credibility to deter any nuclear first strike by an adversary.

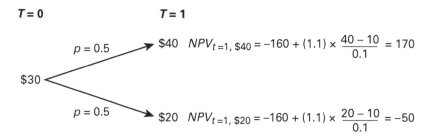

Figure 6.1
Two-stage real optionality.

value of money), but it is more than compensated for by the ability to avoid the scenario of investing in a project, only to see oil prices drop (figure 6.1). A simple calculation reveals that the real optionality component of the project is worth approximately $17.3 million, or more than 20% of the entire value of the project.

If the investment decision was made in $T = 0$, one would expect a positive profit:

$$NPV_{t=0} = -160 + (1.1) \times \frac{\left(\frac{1}{2}40 + \frac{1}{2}20\right) - 10}{0.1} = 60.$$

If the investment decision was made in $T = 1$, the investor would only invest if the price was $40/bbl. Delaying decisions comes at the cost of letting investment capital idle for a period, but it allows the investor to have the benefit of certainty. The NPV of a delayed investment decision is actually higher than that of the project without the deferment option:

$$NPV_{t=1} = \frac{1}{1.1} \times \left(-160 + (1.1) \cdot \frac{40 - 10}{0.1}\right) = 77.27.$$

A More Complex Example

Now let us consider a more complicated and realistic example using a probabilistic tree structure process for the price of oil. Assume the project manager now has the option to irreversibly shut down the project. Beginning with an initial oil price of $50/bbl, we assume that at every subsequent node of the tree, there is a 25% probability that the price will go up, a 50% probability that the price will stay put, and a 25% probability that the price will go down, as in figure 6.2.

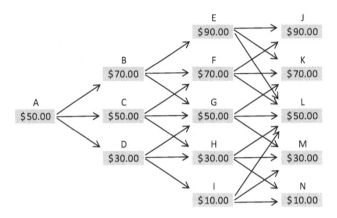

Figure 6.2
Tree structure for oil prices ($ per barrel).

Assuming a discount factor of 0.9, the classic NPV approach would show the project has an NPV of $70.37 million. We can work backward and calculate the free cash flows at each node, as well as the present value (PV) of the subsequent period's cash flow at each node (figure 6.3).

Now let's bring back the optionality of the project operator shutting down *irreversibly*. Since the operator has only one shot at shutting down the project if he or she chooses to do so, the decision must be made carefully. To assess how the operator should exercise the optionality, we must calculate at each node whether it is better to shut down or not. It is worthwhile going through the exercise to replicate the results shown in figure 6.4, which gives the PV at each node and the discounted future expected NPV at that node. At any point where the sum of the two, which captures the entire NPV at that node, turns negative, the operator would prefer to exercise the option to shut down rather than suffer the loss.

But notice that at nodes D and H, the project is not shut down, even though the immediate cash flow is negative, because the expected future profitability is sufficient to outweigh the immediate losses. Meanwhile, at node I, despite the expectation of future profitability if prices ever bounce to node L, the manager would still choose to shut down because the immediate loss is too high.

Using the new theory of investment, we see the true NPV of the project is $75.72 million. Therefore, the pure value of the irreversible shutdown optionality adds an additional $5.35 million to the value of the project.

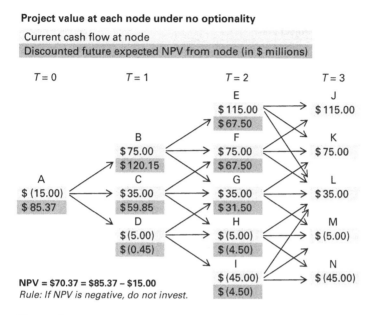

Project value at each node under no optionality

Current cash flow at node
Discounted future expected NPV from node (in $ millions)

$T=0$	$T=1$	$T=2$	$T=3$

E
$115.00
$67.50

B
$75.00
$120.15

F
$75.00
$67.50

J
$115.00

K
$75.00

A
$(15.00)
$85.37

C
$35.00
$59.85

G
$35.00
$31.50

L
$35.00

D
$(5.00)
$(0.45)

H
$(5.00)
$(4.50)

M
$(5.00)

I
$(45.00)
$(4.50)

N
$(45.00)

NPV = $70.37 = $85.37 – $15.00
Rule: If NPV is negative, do not invest.

Figure 6.3
A more realistic optionality example (in $ millions).

Real-World Examples

1 Virtual Gas-Fired Plants

Let's consider a real-world example from a Harvard Business School case study. Enron Europe signed a contract with Eastern Group, a UK electricity generation company, whereby Eastern Group would operate a "virtual gas-fired power plant," having the right to sell electricity in return for natural gas input for ten years. Unlike an oil field or a nuclear power plant, a gas power plant can be turned on or off virtually cost-lessly. Thus, this example features a *reversible* option at every single point in time rather than a one-shot single option. Let's assume that the operator has the ability to shut down or turn on the power plant every half hour.

The key strike price (the price that decides whether to exercise the option to shut down the plant) is the difference between pool electricity prices and the cost of the input gas (sometimes known as the "spark spread"). The history of the spark spread is shown in figure 6.5. The value of this ten-year virtual power plant should be the discounted cash flow of a continuous stream of European call options—indeed,

Project now has option to irreversibly shut down at no abandonment cost at any time after project start

This requires us to work backwards.

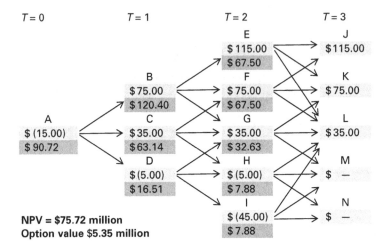

NPV = $75.72 million
Option value $5.35 million

To clarify, the following is the decision tree to shutdown.

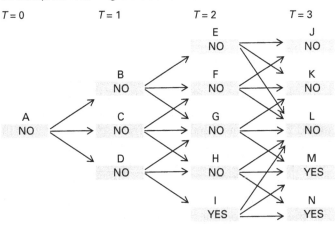

Figure 6.4
Decision tree for shutting down project.

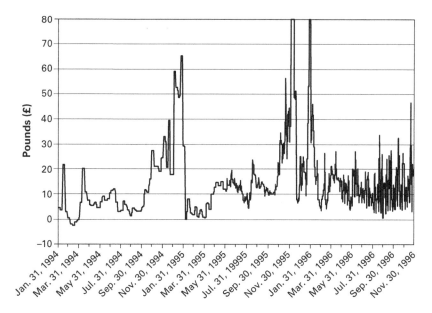

Figure 6.5
Historical spark spread prices.
Source: Benjamin C. Esty, *Modern Project Finance: A Casebook* (New York: Wiley, 2004).

175,200 of them (48 half-hr/d × 365 d/yr × 10 yr)! We can model the behavior of the spark spread as stochastic Brownian motion with mean reversion. However, once we assume mean reversion, there are no quasi-analytic formulas for the price of the European call option as in the Black-Scholes-Merton formula, but the value can be solved numerically with a computer.

2   Storage Facilities

Let's conclude with one final and complex example: an underground oil storage facility. In the case of a storage facility, the optionality value makes up virtually the entirety of the value of the project. This is because the facility, sitting by itself, doesn't actually produce anything of economic value. Its entire value comes from its ability to store and release oil based on market conditions, with the operator taking advantage of periods of lower prices to stock up and periods of high prices to release. This is a very complex optionality as the optionality can be exercised at any point in time, but with constraints. Namely, the storage facility can only release as much oil as there actually is available inside.

There is no option to release, only the option to fill, if the facility is empty.

For simplicity, let's assume the storage facility has no limit to its ability to store oil, but there are costs to filling and withdrawing from it.[3] This adjustment cost is assumed to follow a quadratic form. We also assume that oil prices follow a mean-reverting stochastic Brownian motion known as the Ornstein-Uhlenbeck process:

$$dP_t = \theta\left(\overline{P} - P_t\right)dt + \sigma P dW_t,$$

where θ is the rate of mean reversion, $\overline{P}$ is the long-term mean of the price of oil, and σ is the standard deviation of the Wiener process.

To solve this, we have to use a sophisticated branch of applied mathematics and operations research known as *optimal control theory*. This theory discusses how to solve a surprisingly large variety of optimization problems requiring manipulating various control variables under constraints to try to maximize an objective function (e.g., the discounted NPV of a project) that depends on both the control variable and state variables. Here we have a control variable (how much to fill or release from the reserve) and two state variables, the amount of reserve in the facility and the price of oil. A full review of the theory of optimal control is beyond the scope of this book, but we will try to understand the intuition behind the solution.

Intuitively, a storage operator will want to purchase oil at low prices in order to release the inventory when prices are high. One might think the solution would then be to buy oil whenever prices are below the long-term average and to fill when prices are above the long-term average. After all, prices mean-revert back to that average. This is not a bad starting point.

But first we have to remember that at a reserve level of zero, the storage cannot release any oil, no matter how high the price. Furthermore, the operator also needs to think of the adjustment cost of filling and releasing any oil from the facility, as well as the time value of waiting for prices to mean-revert back to when it is profitable to release the oil.

---

3. Otherwise the problem could result in what is known as a "bang-bang" solution where the optimal strategy is either one of the two extremes—maximum storage or maximum release. We recall that in Hotelling's model, there was no cost to fill or release. Hence prices had to rise at the rate of interest to prevent producers from either dumping or storing the entire supply immediately.

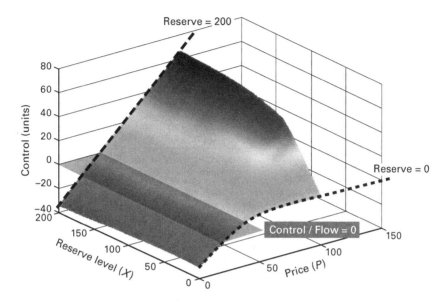

Figure 6.6
Optimal inventory policy (assuming no storage cap).
Source: Author's calculations.

Hence the operator does not start filling up the moment price falls below the long-run average price $(\bar{P})$ but begins purchases when prices fall below a particular point $P^* < \bar{P}$. Figure 6.6 shows the optimal inventory policy at different values of the price and the reserve level.

When the reserve level is very high (e.g., $X = 200$), there is almost no concern about running out of inventory, and the fill/release strategy becomes more or less a linear function of price with the threshold at the long-term average, as in figure 6.7. The higher the price is above the long-term average price, the larger the amount released. Similarly, the lower the price is below the average, the greater the amount filled into the storage facility.

But when the storage facility is empty ($X = 0$), the optimal strategy becomes very different. It looks like a kinked function where fill begins when prices fall below the threshold level, which again is actually below the long-term average price, as shown in figure 6.8. The optimal strategy at intermediate levels of reserve is a smooth transition between these two extremes of the kinked strategy when the reserve is nearly dry and the smooth linear strategy when the reserve is full.

Control variable/
Flow of oil into inventory

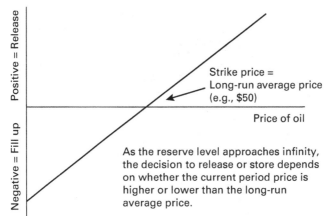

Figure 6.7
Optimal storage policy when inventory approaches infinity.

Control variable/
Flow of oil into inventory

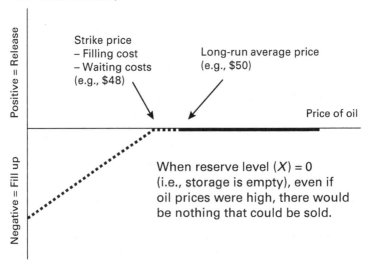

Figure 6.8
Optimal storage policy when inventory is at zero.

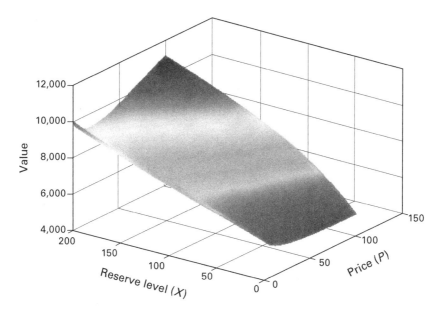

Figure 6.9
Value function of the storage facility.

With the optimal strategy solved, we can then find the actual value of the storage facility. This again depends on the state variables of (1) how much oil is in the facility and (2) where the price of oil is now (figure 6.9). The storage facility naturally becomes more valuable when there is more inventory inside it. But it also becomes more valuable when prices are farther away from the long-term average, since this gives the facility the opportunity to exercise optionality by filling or releasing. This creates a U-shape in the value of the facility that bends outward as the price of oil moves farther away from the mean.

Finally, just as with financial options, the higher the amount of mean reversion θ and volatility σ, the higher will be the real optionality value. Stronger mean reversion means the facility operator can be fairly confident that oil prices will snap back to the mean, making any purchases below the threshold level likely to pay off in the near future. In turn, higher volatility in oil prices means a greater likelihood of having large price swings that create the scenarios of very low or very high prices desired by the storage operator.

At the point when oil prices are at their long-term average and the storage facility is empty, we can put a precise valuation to the storage facility (in this example, $5.3 billion). While this is a highly stylized example requiring heavy theoretical analysis and computation, it does demonstrate the value of the new theory of investment in understanding the true value of real assets that are difficult to value using classic valuation techniques.

7 Commodity Beta: Diversification and Inflation Protection

Although financial exchanges for commodities and portfolio assets linked to commodities—from bullion deposits to mining shares—have been around for centuries, commodities have seen a recent surge in investor interest as an "alternative" asset class.

Academic studies in the 1990s documented the seemingly good risk-versus-return profiles of commodities, low or negative correlations to traditional asset classes and the business cycle, and low cross-commodity correlations. This research inspired many large institutional investors, such as pension funds, sovereign wealth funds, and university endowments (notably Yale University's endowment model under David Swensen), to explore allocating more of their investment portfolios directly to physical commodities and long-only commodity-linked funds. By the time of writing, this investment had grown to massive allocations aggregating to hundreds of billions of dollars, and nearly every large asset manager was making at least some allocation to the commodities sector.

As the populations of the world's advanced and emerging economies age and retire, the financial yields from savings and investment portfolios rather than professional incomes will become ever more important sources of income for households, putting further pressure on asset managers and institutional investors to find ways to deliver that yield. Unsurprisingly, investors have been scouring markets in a search for yield, and interest in alternative assets such as commodities is likely to remain strong.

In this chapter, we discuss the rise of financial instruments linked to commodity markets, the entry of long-term institutional investors as a new class of speculators, and some widely mentioned investment rationales for their exposure, with emphasis on some that have not fared as well as others.

Financialization of Commodities Markets

Earlier chapters discussed the various financial instruments linked to commodity markets, such as futures and options contracts. These have a long and venerable history, dating back to futures contracts developed by Dutch traders in the seventeenth century (including tulip futures during the notorious Dutch tulip bubble in the 1630s) and the Dojima Rice Exchange, established in 1697 in Osaka, Japan. The first modern standardized futures exchange was established to trade grain at the Chicago Board of Trade in 1864. Exchanges subsequently spread to many other commodities, including the first oil-linked futures contract by the New York Mercantile Exchange in 1978.

Since 2002, the rise in trading volume of "paper" oil is indicative of a broader trend. In 1995, financial traders traded paper contracts linked to about one billion barrels of oil every day. By 2012 that number had exploded to more than one *trillion* barrels of oil every day, a thousand times increase (figure 7.1). By contrast, approximately 90 million barrels of *physical* oil are being produced and consumed globally in the spot

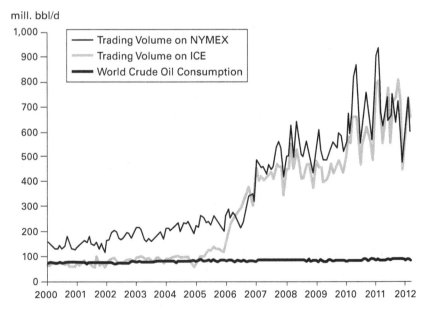

Figure 7.1
Total financial oil trading volume vs. physical volumes, 2000–2012.

USD billions

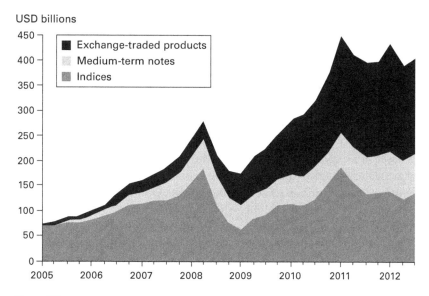

Figure 7.2
Commodity assets under management, 2000–2012. *Sources*: Bloomberg, Barclays Capital.

market every day. In other words, more than 10,000 times as much oil is trading hands financially than is trading physically every day.

Part of this growth was undoubtedly driven by the increasing interest of investors such as hedge funds, institutional investors, and even retail investors in the commodities space. We first concentrate on institutional and retail investors typically interested in long-only allocations to commodities through passive indexes, medium-term notes (MTNs), and exchange-traded products (ETPs). The outstanding value of assets under management (AUM) exceeded $400 billion in early 2011 (figure 7.2).

Part of this increase in value is, of course, being driven by the underlying rise in commodity spot prices, but the increase in these long-only positions represents a major influx of new investment capital into the commodity space. Does it make sense for there to be so much in long-term holdings in commodities?

Commodity Beta and Diversification

A full review of modern portfolio theory (MPT), first articulated by Sharpe and Markowitz, is beyond the scope of this book. As a quick reminder, it assumes investors face a trade-off between the expected return of a portfolio and its risk, often measured as its standard volatility or variance. The capital asset pricing model (CAPM) closes the MPT model by finding that the mean return of any asset, such as stocks, bonds, and so forth, is driven by its beta, or its correlation with the overall fully diversified market portfolio. Assets with a high beta must also have a higher return to compensate investors for their lack of diversification value in reducing overall risk. Any outperformance of an asset not explained by its beta is the elusive "alpha." Such outperformance assigned to alpha might be achieved by taking advantage of arbitrage opportunities or accumulating risk premia.

Inspired by this seminal mean variance framework, investors have come to use the terms "alpha" and "beta" more loosely to refer to any source of uncorrelated and usually ephemeral positive returns from arbitrage versus the portfolio gains that stem from long-term structural exposure to an asset. Much of the challenge to investors is distinguishing between true sources of alpha resulting from mispricing versus being "lucky" with beta.

Is there a beta case to be made for a long-term long-only financial exposure to commodities? The first question is how investors actually gain said exposure. The vast majority of passive index investments, medium-term notes (MTNs), and exchange-traded products (ETPs) follow some variation of the "rolling" strategy described in chapter 4, whereby the investor takes a long position in a futures contract at F_t^{t+1}, exits it immediately before expiration at the future spot price S_{t+1}, then uses the proceeds to buy another futures contract, which starts the cycle again.

As seen before, the performance of this rolling strategy can be divided into two components, the spot return, $\dfrac{S_{t+1}}{S_t}$, and the inverse roll return, $\dfrac{F_t^{t+1}}{S_t}$:

$$\log\left(\frac{S_{t+1}}{F_t^{t+1}}\right) = \log\left(\frac{S_{t+1}}{S_t}\right) - \log\left(\frac{F_t^{t+1}}{S_t}\right).$$

If the markets are risk neutral and there is no risk premium, then $F_t^{t+1} = E[S_{t+1}]$, and this rolling strategy will on average result in zero returns. Any consistent outperformance comes from the alpha associated with reaping the risk premia by providing economic insurance to commercial hedgers, not from any beta exposure to the underlying spot returns of the commodity. (We discuss the alpha from this spread alpha in the next chapter.) But the entire concept of relying on rolling strategies to provide beta exposure rests on shaky theoretical ground. To the degree it works in practice it is because, as we saw earlier, futures markets do a terrible job of predicting future spot prices, and spot price returns swamp any roll returns. We return to this topic in the next chapter.

But suppose the investor does find a financial product that provides a relatively unadulterated exposure to the spot return, such as through holding physical storage, purchasing farmland, or leasing undeveloped energy acreage. Is a long-term exposure to this source of beta desirable? To answer this question, we need to understand the underlying economic relationship between commodity markets and whatever other asset classes the investor is holding in his or her portfolio, such as stocks or bonds.

We discussed the relationship between commodities and fundamental demand and supply factors in previous chapters. Commodity demand is driven by global demand factors, such as the business cycle and structural economic growth. The impressive but resource-intensive growth by emerging economies, particularly China and India, has underpinned an impressive spot market return across many commodities markets since the beginning of the twenty-first century.

In other words, commodities can offer indirect exposure to the rise of emerging markets and the aspirations of millions of newly middle-class households with resource-intensive consumption patterns, such as a taste for private automobiles and beefsteaks.

But this is a *positively correlated* relationship: stronger economic growth lifts both equity markets and commodity prices together. Presumably investors seeking diversification are looking for negative or at least neutral relationships to traditional equity asset classes. At best, what they are gaining is a *substitute* rather than a *complement* to emerging market equities and bonds. This may still be valuable, but it is a far cry from the idea of commodities as a source of diversification or low or negative beta compared to other asset classes.

In fact, even for developed market equities, such as the U.S. S&P 500 total return index, the returns look positively correlated to commodity price indexes, such as the popular S&P Goldman Sachs Commodity Index (GSCI) benchmark, particularly around areas of global demand

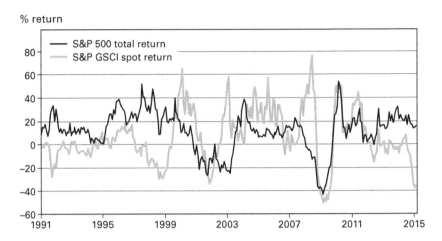

Figure 7.3
S&P 500 total return vs. GSCI spot return, 1991–2016,

shocks such as the 2009 global recession and ensuing financial crisis (figure 7.3).

Furthermore, unlike commodities, equities generate continued economic value; companies try to generate value through the provision of goods and services to consumers. The value of companies may see long-term continued appreciation through technological growth and profits from market share. But commodities are just static goods, and, as discussed in previous chapters, their long-term level is stationary despite long super-cycles up and down. The long-term return of a long-only allocation to commodities is zero (or even negative, if technological progress causes a commodity to become obsolete).

This positive linkage between commodity demand and economic growth, on the one hand, and no long-term return on the other suggests that commodities are *not* an ideal asset class from a diversification perspective.

However, there may be another rationale for investing in commodity beta: to protect against political shocks. Here the diversification argument is more straightforward. Political shocks that cause commodity prices to rise, for example, a hot war that disrupts supply, may also depress economic growth and equities as companies and households face higher commodity prices. In particular, a geopolitical tail event that depresses equity prices may in turn cause commodities to spike. We discuss geopolitical tail events in chapter 9.

Commodity Beta and Inflation Protection

Another rationale for seeking a beta allocation to commodities is to protect against inflation. Inflation is defined as a general rise in nominal prices for a broad basket of goods and services in an economy. This basket includes commodities consumed widely by households and companies, such as food and energy.

Economists often distinguish between *headline inflation*, which captures the entire consumption basket, and *core inflation*, isolated to only the basket of non-food and non-energy goods and services. Why does this help? First, by removing noise from the frequently volatile food and energy subcomponents, core inflation can provide a more stable and meaningful assessment of the price stability of the underlying economy.

Second, because core inflation reflects the pricing decisions of a wider category of firms, movements in core inflation are a more useful predictor of future inflation than are changes in headline inflation. Partially for this reason, core inflation is the inflation metric most widely watched by central banks in determining monetary policy. Doing otherwise would result in a hypersensitive monetary policy.

Inflation reduces the real purchasing power of any nominally denominated financial assets such as cash, stocks, and (non-inflation-linked) bonds. This real wealth destruction should be of great concern to investors. A portfolio exposure to commodities, a major driver of headline inflation (and particularly unexpected inflation), can thus serve as a financial hedge against inflation.

To assess the efficacy of commodity beta as an inflation hedge, we must first explore the relationship between commodity prices and broader core and headline inflation. First, as mentioned above, commodities have a straightforward direct presence in broad consumption baskets. In the United States, for example, housing is the largest component of the CPI consumption basket (figure 7.4). But transportation and food costs, which are closely linked to energy and agricultural commodity prices, are also substantial. The U.S. Bureau of Labor Statistics (BLS) calculated that commodities account for as much as 41% of headline inflation, with the largest drivers being food (14%) and energy (8%) in 2017.

It is important to note that as substantial as food and energy expenses are to the average consumer in a developed economy, they are dwarfed by their importance to consumers in emerging and developing

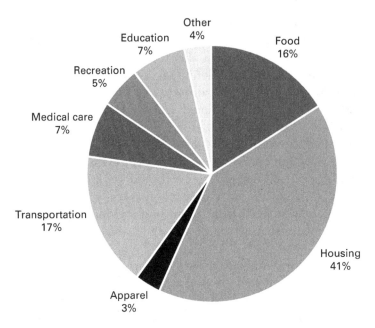

Figure 7.4
Components of U.S. Consumer Price Index (2015).

economies. The importance of food expenses alone runs anywhere
from 25% to as high as 75% for certain sub-Saharan African nations.
The economic distress that results from high food prices in the poorest
nations has made food security a top issue on the international policy
agenda. Governments in the developing world are particularly sensitive to high food prices because those prices can spill over into the
political arena, galvanizing discontent against the incumbent regime.
Many of the simmering tensions that led to the Arab Spring and regime
change in Tunisia, Libya, and Egypt can be traced to anger over food
costs, as well as frustration over stagnant economies and corrupt
regimes.

But in addition to the direct presence of commodities in consumption baskets, there are also more pernicious ways that commodity price
inflation can indirectly affect even non-commodity-linked core inflation, such as when firms increase prices for goods and services because
of higher input costs. For example, even though a household living in
an apartment building may not be directly consuming copper, the
landlord may raise rents because of higher maintenance costs when
copper prices rise. This pass-through from headline commodity prices

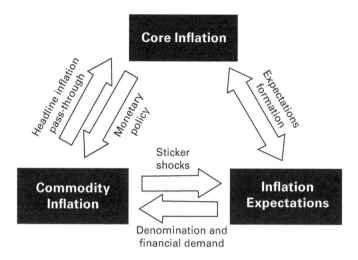

Figure 7.5
Relationships among commodity inflation, core inflation, and inflation expectations.

to the core inflation basket is one mechanism by which commodity prices might affect broader inflation as well as inflation expectations.

This complicated three-way relationship among commodities, core inflation, and expectations is captured in the triangle shown in figure 7.5.

We have already discussed the direct pass-through from commodities to core inflation. Economic policy makers—in particular central banks—may respond to higher core inflation levels with contractionary policies such as raising interest rates. Raising rates slows economic growth and depresses real demand for commodities.

Furthermore, sudden increases in food, energy, and other commodity prices may also affect market expectations of future general inflation. When economic agents begin to expect high levels of inflation, it can become a self-fulfilling prophecy. This cycle can even occur when there is slack in the real economy, as any student of the 1970s oil price shocks and resulting stagflationary unhinging of inflation expectations in the United States can testify.

In turn, higher inflation and inflation expectations can drive significant appreciation in nominal commodity prices. This happens for two reasons: first, because inflation means the real value of the denominating currency (typically the U.S. dollar) is depreciating, and second, as a result of higher financial demand for commodities as an inflation hedge, notably for precious metals.

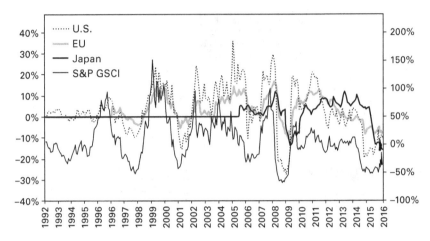

Figure 7.6
Energy inflation for selected economies and the S&P GSCI Energy Sub-Index, % year-over-year returns, 1992–2016.
Source: Bloomberg.

How well do commodity indexes track consumer inflation in practice? Figures 7.6 and 7.7 show the recent energy component of consumer inflation in the United States, the EU, and Japan compared to the Energy Sub-Index, which tracks the energy subcomponent of the S&P GSCI. As we can see, the index tracked headline energy inflation quite well, with correlations ranging from 40% to 50% for Japan to as high as 70% to 80% for the United States and the EU.

However, the S&P GSCI Agriculture Sub-Index does a much poorer job of tracking food inflation for the same economies, with correlations negative for Japan (figures 7.8 and 7.9).

It is possible the difference may reflect weaker pass-through of raw agricultural commodity prices into retail food prices due to greater pricing wedges introduced by intermediate processors and distributors in the food sector compared to the energy sector. It may also be driven by different commodity preference baskets. A heavily rice-based food index in Japan may not be as well tracked by an index that tracks global corn and wheat prices.

To conclude, commodities are a significant source of direct inflation to consumers and, given their substantial correlation to overall inflation indices, investing directly in commodities can provide some (imperfect) protection against inflation. But in the next section, we shall

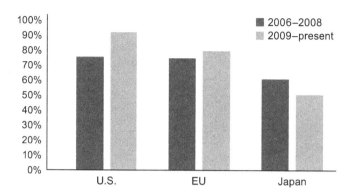

Figure 7.7
Spot energy prices and energy subcomponent inflation correlations.
Source: Bloomberg.

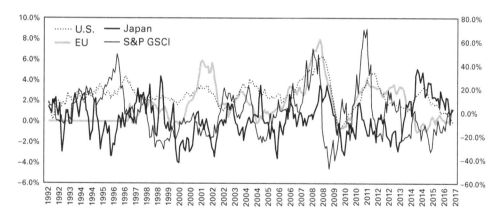

Figure 7.8
Food inflation for selected economies and the S&P GSCI Food Sub-Index, % year-over-year returns, 1992–present.
Source: Bloomberg.

discuss the more powerful linkages between commodity prices and *unexpected* inflation shocks.

Expected versus Unexpected Inflation

We have discussed the relationship between commodity prices and the commodity-linked sources of headline inflation. What about the rest of core inflation unrelated directly to food and energy prices? In fact, in so far as any inflation that has already been built into expectations,

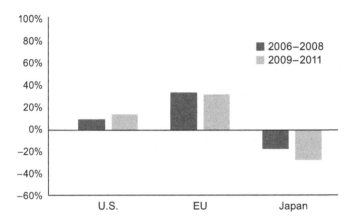

Figure 7.9
Spot food prices and food subcomponent inflation correlations.
Source: Bloomberg.

companies and bond issuers should have already (in theory) reflected them in their business and pricing decisions. For example, consider a zero-coupon bond that should pay $110 in face value one year from now, and assume that the nominal interest rate was zero (no time value of money). If investors already expect that there should be 10% nominal inflation throughout the year, they would correctly recognize that $110 one year from now is worth $100 in real terms, and this bond should already be priced at $100. Only cash would see a true erosion of real value from any expected inflation.

And should problems in the ability of companies and bond markets prevent a perfect readjustment of asset prices to absorb expected inflation, fear not! Many governments have begun issuing inflation-linked securities, such as the U.S. Treasury Inflation-Protected Securities (TIPS) and the UK's Inflation-linked Gilts. These securities represent the most direct means by which investors can protect against expected inflation, as either the bond's coupons or the principal repayments are explicitly linked to some common measure of inflation (e.g., the U.S. CPI). Even many emerging economies have begun issuing instruments linked to inflation.

The problem with inflation-linked securities is that while they serve as an excellent hedge against *expected* inflation, market expectations of future inflation do not necessarily capture the actual realization of inflation. In other words, investors also face significant *unexpected* infla-

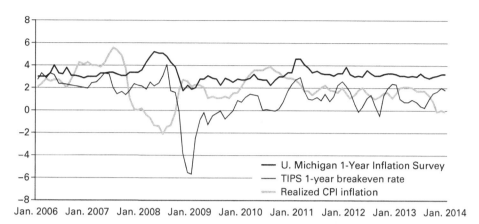

Figure 7.10
Inflation expectations vs. realized inflation.

tion shocks. Figure 7.10 compares various measures of inflationary expectations, such as the University of Michigan's surveys of inflation or the amount of inflation priced in by the one-year TIPS market compared to the actual realization of U.S. CPI inflation one year hence. It is clear that markets did a rather terrible job of foreseeing realized inflation, especially during the global recession of 2008–2009.

Here is where commodity beta investment can truly shine as an inflation hedge, because commodity-tracking indices often prove highly correlated to unexpected inflationary shocks. In 2007, realized CPI inflation proved much higher than earlier forecasts had expected, in part because of record-high oil prices. Ironically, by the time inflationary expectations caught up in 2008, actual inflation had plunged as a result of the global economic crisis. A holder of TIPS would have had almost no protection against these inflationary oscillations.

Furthermore, some commodities are not actually commodities in the traditional sense but are prized as stores of financial value, such as gold, diamonds, and other precious materials. They also perform excellently as real hedges against inflation, especially in hyperinflation scenarios in which other market assets may do poorly as a result of economic mismanagement. The precious metals are a special category more akin to currencies driven by purely financial factors such as inflation, real interest rates, and investor demand rather than they are like commodities whose price is driven by supply and demand fundamentals.

Commodity Beta

To conclude, despite the vast increase of portfolio investment and inter-est into purely financial long-only exposure to commodities, the "beta" case for commodity portfolio investment rests on relatively shaky grounds. In terms of uncorrelated or negatively correlated diversifica-tion complementing traditional equity and bond asset classes, com-modity beta does not appear to perform particularly well, even against developed market equities. Furthermore, the long-term returns on commodities are zero or negative. The outstanding returns of commod-ity indices in the 2000s is actually a function of a supercyclic upswing in equilibrium prices due to emerging market economic growth. This outperformance should not be misconstrued as a permanent source of beta outperformance.

However, commodity beta may hold some value to long-term inves-tors by providing a valuable source of protection against inflation. This includes not only the direct inflationary exposure to commodities—such as food and energy—but especially protection against unexpected inflationary shocks, a source of portfolio risk that other asset classes, including inflation-protection securities, struggle to protect against.

8   Commodity Alpha: Risk Premia

In the previous chapter we discussed the various rationales for investors seeking commodity beta exposure for diversification and inflation hedging purposes. In this chapter we discuss some sources of commodity alpha, or the uncorrelated outperformance generated by investing cleverly in commodity markets. In particular, we shall focus our discussion on any systemic portfolio outperformance generating by reaping risk premia embedded across the futures curve for commodities.

Of course, there is also the outperformance generated by taking advantage of arbitrage opportunities and potential mispricing in commodity markets. The entire industry of hedge funds, private equity funds, commodity traders, and other speculators is devoted to searching for these market anomalies to exploit. Massive amounts of resources are poured into developing sophisticated quantitative and qualitative methods in search of this source of alpha, sometimes with considerable success. To be successful at this form of speculation requires a superior understanding of commodity markets to better predict the behavior of future prices (at least better than the understanding of one's peers in the market).

But arbitrating market mispricings ultimately drives prices back to their "true" equilibrium levels, and hence any source of arbitrage alpha is, by its nature, ephemeral. By contrast, the potential outperformance gained from reaping positive risk premia should always exist while there is hedging demand seeking insurance against commodity price volatility.

Risk Premia Revisited

This section quickly reviews risk premia and the mechanics of their relationship to spot returns and roll returns, discussed in chapter 4.

Risk premia are defined as the price spreads between futures prices F_t^{t+k} and *expected future* spot prices $E_t(S_{t+k})$. The risk premium comes from the physical producers and consumers who are willing to pay a premium to offload commodity price risk, which can dramatically affect their revenue and cost profiles, onto others.

For example, an airline company concerned about a potential rise in petroleum product prices may choose to hedge by purchasing oil futures. To hedge that risk, the company will pay a premium over expected spot prices to guarantee a ceiling to its oil bill. Similarly, a corn farmer fearful of a plunge in corn prices may decide to sell a portion of her crop at a discount from expected spot prices in return for price security and peace of mind. Thus risk premia can be considered economic "insurance commissions" paid by physical hedgers to investors to assume the risk of the offsetting financial position.

The "normal" short positions of hedging producers and the "normal" long positions of hedging consumers may naturally offset each other, but the offset is rarely perfect. For example, figure 8.1 shows that the net long positions of money managers and the net short positions of producer or users reflect each other, but not exactly. This imperfection opens a window for the existence of nonzero risk premia for financial speculators to exploit.

Let's review the simple strategy whereby a speculator purchases a futures contract F_t^{t+k} at time t for delivery k periods later. At that time, he plans to sell the futures contract at the future spot price, S_{t+k}. The expected gross total return on this buy-and-hold strategy is:

$$1 + R_t = \frac{S_{t+k}}{F_t^{t+k}} = \frac{S_{t+k}}{S_t} \times \frac{S_t}{F_t^{t+k}}.$$

Taking natural logs, we can decompose the total return into two components: the expected spot return and the inverse of the roll return. The first term captures the future spot return of the commodity. The second term, which we call the roll return, captures the slope or the degree of backwardation of the futures curve at the time of investment:

$$r_t \equiv \log(1 + R_t) = \log\left(\frac{S_{t+k}}{S_t}\right) - \log(\frac{F_t^{t+k}}{S_t}).$$

Under risk neutrality, futures prices should equal expected future spot prices: $F_t^{t+k} = E_t[S_{t+k}]$. Then the expected return of the hold-and-

Contracts (thous.)

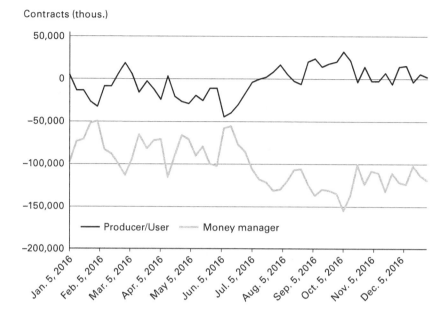

Figure 8.1
Net positions of producer/users and money managers for CBOT wheat (in thousands of contracts).

roll strategy should be zero, as the roll return cancels out the expected future spot return:

$$r_t = \log\left(\frac{S_{t+k}}{S_t}\right) - \log\left(\frac{E_t[S_{t+k}]}{S_t}\right) \approx 0.$$

Only when there are systematic risk premia in the futures curve can there be systematic outperformance of this strategy gaining risk premia. And in practice, there do seem to be large amounts of risk premia in futures markets.

A simple way to confirm this empirically is to compare spot returns, $\frac{S_{t+1}}{S_t}$, and roll returns, $\frac{F_{t+1}}{S_t}$. If there were no risk premia, roll returns would equal (at least on average) future spot price returns. But spot returns and roll returns tend to track each other very poorly, as figure 8.2 shows for the case of West Texas Intermediate (WTI) crude oil. If anything, they have been negatively correlated.

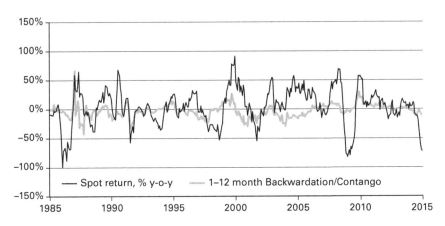

Figure 8.2
Percent year-over-year spot returns and one-year futures spread for WTI crude oil.

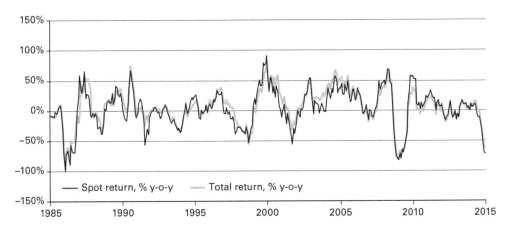

Figure 8.3
Percent year-over-year spot and total returns for WTI crude oil.

This risk premium can be exploited by speculators to gain expected positive portfolio performance, at the cost of bearing commodity risk away from hedgers.

But a corollary of the fact that roll returns and spot returns do not track each other well is that the performance of passive roll-and-hold indexes such as the S&P Goldman Sachs Commodity Index (GSCI) actually track theoretical spot returns closely. There is almost no visible difference between a roll-and-hold strategy and the spot return for WTI crude oil (figure 8.3).

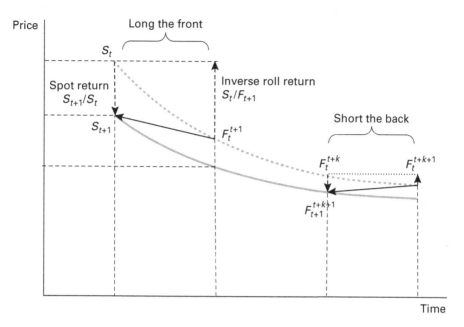

Figure 8.4
Mechanics of beta neutralization using calendar spreads.

This is great news for investors seeking beta exposure to commodities. But what about speculators who are just looking for risk premia–driven alpha, not the beta? One way to "neutralize" this beta component is by adopting a counterweight exposure at a different portion of the futures curve. This practice has been adopted for many "smart" alpha commodity products offered by financial institutions.

Suppose a speculator would like to go long the one-period futures contract at the front end of the futures curve as he or she believes there is excess backwardation driven by risk premia (the same logic would apply, only in reverse, if the investor felt there was excess contango). However, the speculator would like to neutralize any exposure to the spot return, and does so by taking an inverse short position at the "back" end of the futures curve for contracts with delivery dates further in the future (figure 8.4). In short, the investor is doing the same hold-and-roll strategy discussed above in the front, but is simultaneously shorting the same hold-and-roll strategy at the back end of the curve.

Mechanically, the speculator's total return would now be the following:

$$r_t^k \equiv \log\left(\frac{S_{t+1}}{F_t^{t+1}}\right) - \log\left(\frac{F_{t+1}^{t+k+1}}{F_t^{t+k+1}}\right).$$

This expression can be decomposed into the analogues to the spot and roll returns seen previously:

$$r_t^k = \left[\log\left(\frac{S_{t+1}}{S_t}\right) - \log\left(\frac{F_t^{t+1}}{S_t}\right)\right] - \left[\log\left(\frac{F_{t+1}^{t+k+1}}{F_t^{t+k}}\right) - \log\left(\frac{F_t^{t+k+1}}{F_t^{t+k}}\right)\right].$$

With a little algebraic rearranging, we see the total return of this beta-neutralized alpha strategy can also be divided into a "parallel" shift term and a "convexity" term:

$$r_t^k = \left[\log\left(\frac{S_{t+1}}{S_t}\right) - \log\left(\frac{F_{t+1}^{t+k+1}}{F_t^{t+k}}\right)\right] - \left[\log\left(\frac{F_t^{t+1}}{S_t}\right) - \log\left(\frac{F_t^{t+k+1}}{F_t^{t+k}}\right)\right].$$

The first term collects all of the "beta" risk components of the long and short handles of the alpha strategy. Ideally, this would be neutralized as any spot returns, $\frac{S_{t+1}}{S_t}$, at the front are offset by parallel movements by futures prices at the back, $\frac{F_{t+1}^{t+k+1}}{F_t^{t+k}}$. We call this the "parallel" term, and under ideal circumstances, it should be roughly zero.

The second term compares the relative slopes of the futures curve at the front, $\frac{F_t^{t+1}}{S_t}$, with those at the rear, $\frac{F_t^{t+k+1}}{F_t^{t+k}}$. In other words, this term captures the convexity of the futures curve, or the change in the slope of the curve as one moves across the calendar dates of delivery.

The efficacy of this alpha strategy depends on two complementary factors: first, the presence of convexity in the futures curve, and second, how much the futures curve likes to move by "parallel" movements up or down rather than with changes to its slope. If the futures curve moves in parallel, the short position on futures at the back end of the curve effectively neutralizes the spot returns of the long position, and the convexity term delivers any risk premia to the speculator.

Empirically, it appears that for some commodities, the futures curve does like to move in parallel, and any convexity may be a sign of risk premia. A simple principal components analysis (PCA) suggests that such parallel movements can explain a significant share of the variation of many commodities (figure 8.5):

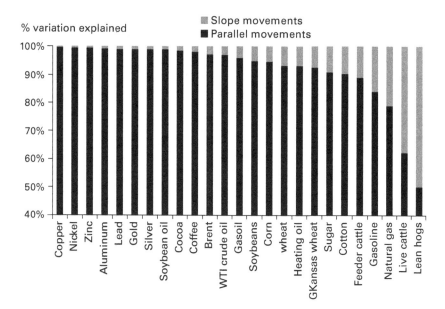

Figure 8.5
Price variation explained by parallel movements vs. changes to slope.

The industrial base and precious metals feature the greatest degree of parallel shifts, followed by certain soft commodities, such as coffee and cocoa. Meanwhile, energy commodities, such as gasoline and natural gas, as well as livestock commodities such as cattle and hogs, see a much higher fraction of their overall price variation driven by slope changes. It is likely that the highly perishable soft commodities require significant slope movements to compensate storage operators for the expense of storage, as the Working-Kaldor theory would suggest.

Furthermore, for a variety of reasons, producers, consumers, and money managers tend to compartmentalize themselves along different segments of the calendar. In the oil market, physical consumers such as airlines, refiners, storage operators, and the like, tend to cluster around the front end of the futures curve (along with passive institutional investors), where liquidity is high. Meanwhile, large producers and resource-dependent states and state-owned enterprises (notably the Mexican Ministry of Finance), with their longer horizons, tend to hedge more of their books along the back end of the curve, often in large and lumpy increments. Figure 8.6 shows the amount of open interest along the WTI crude oil curve, with a high degree of financial interest concentrated at the front end of the curve.

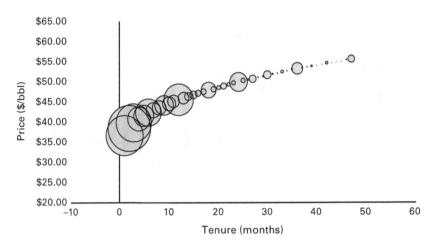

Figure 8.6
Prices and open interest segmentation along the WTI crude oil futures curve.
Source: Bloomberg.

Our beta-neutralization strategy may be reaping double the risk premia by selling and providing liquidity facing the long hedges of consumers at the front portion of the curve while buying and again providing liquidity for the short hedges of producers at the back end.

Conclusion

The continued interest by financial investors in the commodity space can be seen in the dizzying array of commodity-linked portfolio products offered by the financial industry. But the prospective investor should not be fooled. The success and popularity of many of these alpha strategies should not disguise the fact that they are not a "free lunch" but rather the earning of risk premia by financial investors for assuming risk from their counterparts. Understanding the drivers of this risk premium and how it percolates through the anatomy of alpha strategies is essential for more intelligent and efficient portfolio construction.

There is no silver bullet when it comes to calendar alpha, and each method must be weighed according to its own merits. Navigating commodity markets in the context of shifting demand and supply fundamentals idiosyncratic to each commodity, investor repositioning, changing storage dynamics, and so on is essential for the ultimate success of the intelligent investor.

Module IV: Other Topics

In this final module we delve into various special topics not covered in the earlier modules, including distortions introduced into markets by geopolitics, how to think about regulation of financial markets for commodities to improve market efficiency, and a survey of the economics of electricity markets.

In chapter 9 we discuss various political distortions introduced into energy markets, including the actions of state-owned oil and gas companies, cartel behavior by OPEC, the provision fuel subsidies, pipeline geopolitics, and energy security issues.

In chapter 10 we address the topic of financial regulation. We begin by discussing the goals of financial regulation and the peculiar challenges presented by commodity markets, then discuss various regulatory mechanisms.

In chapter 11 we cover markets for electricity, which by their nature create special features such as real-time demand and supply matching and markets for congestion and capacity not seen in traditional commodity markets.

9 Geopolitics and Commodities

For most of this book, commodity markets have been assumed to be driven largely by economic factors and grounded in supply-and-demand fundamentals, though subject to informational opacity and speculative mania. However, the sad reality is that in many commodity market segments, politics can trump economics, and markets are heavily distorted by politically motivated factors. In this chapter we discuss some of the major political distortions affecting markets, particularly markets in energy:

- Resource scarcity and security
- Resource nationalism and national oil and gas companies
- Commodity producer cartels
- Energy subsidies
- Pipeline geopolitics

This list is not meant to be exhaustive or comprehensive. Another book (and there are many) would be needed to do justice to the complex relationship between commodity markets and the political systems in which they are embedded.

Resource Scarcity and Security

The terms "resource scarcity," "energy security," "peak oil," or "energy independence" appear frequently in the political discourse of many countries. Because of the high dependence of modern economies on commodities such as oil and food, there is a constant fear of the vulnerability of society should such commodity supplies become disrupted or exhausted (figure 9.1). Dystopian visions of a post-apocalyptic society in which resources have run out (the topic of countless science

Figure 9.1
The *Economist* magazine proclaims the end of the oil age.
Source: Reproduced by permission of The Economist Newspaper Ltd., London (Oct. 23, 2003).

fiction novels and films) have been potently exploited by fear-mongering politicians to drive policy.

These Malthusian visions of resource scarcity, however, have been repeatedly disproved throughout history by the forces of economics incentivizing the search for new commodity supplies and substitutes. Nevertheless, economic (remember the low price elasticities!) and political sensitivities have made the provision of "resource security" a universally desired public good demanded of all modern governments by their constituents (figure 9.2).

"Resource security" is a term that is used loosely in many contexts but can be roughly defined as the provision of affordable, reliable,

Figure 9.2
Soviet propaganda poster: "Soviets and Electrification Are the Foundation of the New World!"

accessible, and sustainable sources of resources. These various factors are in constant tension with each other. Yet the ultimately fallacious nature of many arguments around resource security should not cause us to underestimate their political potency or the very real political distortions currently existing in many commodity markets.

Indeed, in many ways, some of the most cataclysmic human events were caused by fears around resource security. World War II can be partially viewed as driven by overly simplistic views of resource scarcity in Nazi Germany (*Lebensraum*) and imperial Japan (*Southern Resource Area*), whose leaders thought the direct military conquest and control of energy, food, land, rubber, tin, and other commodity resources

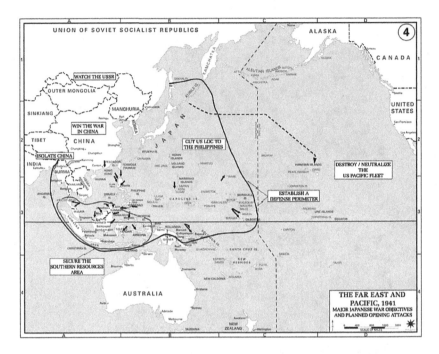

Figure 9.3
Securing the "Southern Resources Area" was a key component of Imperial Japan's 1941 war objectives.

was an existential prerequisite for the survival and eventual triumph of their nation or race. Certainly, those views shaped the direction of their military campaigns, and the loss of oil supplies proved to be a major and possibly even decisive factor in the ultimate defeat of the Axis powers.

The postwar economic experience emphasizes the intellectual bankruptcy of these "zero-sum" or "mercantilist" views of resource security. Relatively resource-poor nations such as Germany, Japan, South Korea, China, and India (among others) have seen remarkable economic postwar growth, while resource-rich nations like the former Soviet Union, the Congo, and Venezuela have lagged. This is in part thanks to the free flow of goods and services in the global trading system, which allows resource-poor economies to trade their output for commodities.

Yet the intellectual descendants of these views, whether under the rubric of "peak oil" or "energy independence," remain embedded in the popular discourse today. Those calling for U.S. "energy indepen-

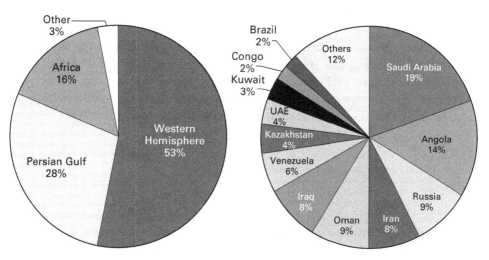

Figure 9.4
U.S. vs. Chinese dependence on foreign oil.
Sources: Left, U.S. Energy Information Administration, *Petroleum Supply Monthly,* February 2013. Right, Global Trade information Services, *FACTS Global Energy.*

dence" demand the United States wean itself off dependence on imported "foreign" oil. This political sound bite is based on a misconception that the U.S. energy market is autarkic and nonintegrated with the rest of world. In fact, the United States is relatively less dependent on imports, particularly on unreliable Middle Eastern imports, than China, especially after the onset of the U.S. unconventional hydrocarbon revolution (figure 9.4).

But ironically, this dependence means virtually nothing from a resource security perspective. As oil is a fungible commodity and its markets are globally integrated, U.S. and Chinese consumers face the same (pre-tax) global price of oil, no matter what their import dependence may be. Any difference would cause the free market to shift supplies to arbitrage that price spread.

The example of the 1973 OPEC embargo is instructive. In a gesture of support to fellow Arabic nation Egypt during the Yom Kippur War with Israel, the Arab members of OPEC categorized countries into friendly, neutral, and unfriendly status. Unfriendly countries such as the United States and the Netherlands that remained publicly supportive of Israel would face a complete embargo. Meanwhile, friendly countries such as the United Kingdom, France, and Japan (which did a rather craven about-face) would enjoy full access. This distinction did not help the "friendly" countries become more immune to the oil shock; *all* faced the same price hike. A similar circumstance occurred during the more recent Libyan revolution in 2011. Most Libyan oil goes to Europe, but American and European consumers faced the same price increases as supplies that would have otherwise have gone to the U.S. market were diverted to Europe (box 9.1).

Box 9.1
Fat Tails, Power Laws, and Oil Markets

Geopolitical shocks to oil markets, such as the 1973 OPEC embargo, the 1979 Iranian Revolution, or the 1980 Iran-Iraq War, are often blamed for causing extreme fat-tailed events in the behavior of oil markets. But recent research suggests that these are not isolated "black swan" events but part of a broader pattern of non-Gaussian "power law" distributions seen in an extraordinary variety of economic and physical contexts, such as income distributions, the size of cities, executive pay, the frequency of words, and the metabolic rate of biological organizations.

The Gaussian distribution, also known as the normal distribution or the "bell curve," is also universal in the natural and social sciences. Its ubiquity is driven by the central limit theorem, which posits that, under certain regularity conditions, the normalized average of random variables drawn from any probability distribution converges to that of a Gaussian distribution. Popular financial models such as the Black-Scholes-Merton formula or the Sharpe-Markowitz mean-variance model typically assume normal or Gaussian probability distributions for price returns. These have "thin" tails, with the cumulative probability for large σ events declining rapidly to zero.

By contrast, power-lawed or Pareto distributions have thick tails, with the probability of large σ events declining, as the name suggests, according to a power function. A power law, also known as a scaling law, is a relation of the type $Y = kx^{-\zeta}$, where Y and X are variables of interest, ζ is called the power law exponent, and k is some constant. (A power law with $\zeta = 1$ is sometimes known as Zipf's law.)

Empirically, to precisely measure the degree of non-Gaussian fat tails in crude oil markets, we need a very large number of data points to get sufficient observations of large σ events, which by definition are extremely rare. Figure 9.5 plots the cumulative probability of large σ return events plotted on a logarithmic scale using a database of more than 47 million observations of high-frequency prices for WTI crude oil prices from the beginning of 2000 to the end of 2008.

Box 9.1 (continued)

If crude oil price returns were indeed power-lawed rather than Gauss-ian-distributed, then the probability that oil price returns exceeds an amount x standard deviations away from the mean should be a *log-linear* function of the natural log of x:

$$\ln[P(r > x)] = -\zeta \ln(x) + \text{cons}\tan t.$$

As we can see from figure 9.5, for return events exceeding two stan-dard deviations (two sigma or higher) from the mean, a log-linear func-tion with a power law coefficient of about 2.7 does an excellent job of fitting the empirical distribution of oil price returns, including one 65-sigma event!

Hence, far from being isolated exceptions to the normal Gaussian distribution, oil markets feature highly power-lawed distributions in their tails. Despite their analytical tractability and popularity, economists are reexamining the assumptions of standard Gaussian behavior for the prices of many commodities and other financial assets.

Indeed, if the United States truly wished to strengthen its energy security and build some resilience against foreign oil shocks and other political externalities, imposing higher Pigovian taxes on imported oil would help. The imposition of a tax would reduce the volatility of after-tax prices faced by consumers and businesses, helping them with investment planning and financial decision making. It would divert tax revenue toward the U.S. Treasury instead of toward the coffers of oil exporters, some of them geopolitical adversaries, such as Russia or Iran. It would also economically stimulate domestic production, energy efficiency, and the search for technological substitutes. Any additional financial burden caused by higher after-tax fuel prices could be offset by vouchers for lower-income households and reduced income or cor-porate taxes. Yet this proposal remains politically dead on arrival as no politician wants to advocate for higher headline prices at the fuel pump. This economic tone deafness represents one of the greatest missed opportunities by U.S. policy makers.

Of course, markets do best at ensuring resource security if goods and services can move freely as competitive economic forces dictate. It is when political factors prevent this free movement that concerns over resource security are justified. For example, during wartime, military blockades and embargoes can physically cut off supplies from markets no matter the economic logic. Indeed, blockades were a key military

Cumulative probability *Prob (X > x)*

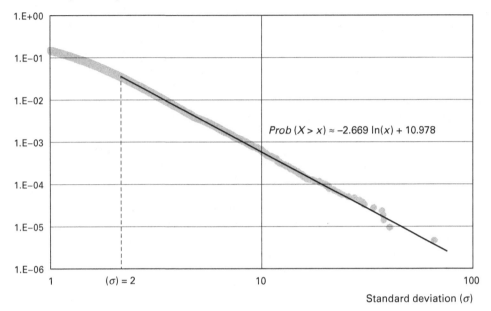

Figure 9.5
Cumulative probabilities of high sigma events in crude oil price returns on a logarithmic scale.

strategy used with remarkable success against Germany in World War I and Japan in World War II. Hence the world's navies constantly monitor and patrol maritime chokepoints, such as the Strait of Hormuz or the Strait of Malacca, to maintain the free flow of oil supplies against any threats (figure 9.6).

But even in peacetime, economic forces may not be given free reign. We discuss some of the most egregious distortions in energy markets, including the rise of state-owned resource companies, next.

Resource Nationalism and National Energy Companies

Perhaps the most extreme yet often underappreciated political distortion in the global energy market is the lack of free competitive access for the bulk of the world's proven (and cheapest) oil and natural gas reserves. Instead, the development of these reserves is restricted to state-owned enterprises, also known as national oil (and gas) companies (NOCs).

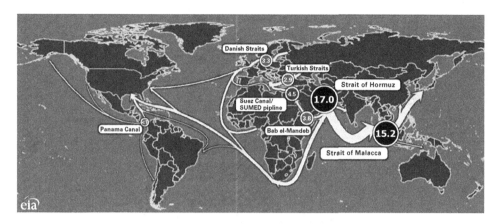

Figure 9.6
Maritime oil flow chokepoints: daily transit volumes.
Source: U.S. Energy Information Administration (EIA).

This fact is surprisingly obscure to the public, which tends to think of the major international oil companies (IOCs) such as ExxonMobil or British Petroleum as "Big Oil." But in fact, in terms of holdings of reserves, the IOCs are minnows compared to NOCs such as Saudi Aramco, the National Iranian Oil Company (NIOC), Venezuela's PdVSA, and Russia's Gazprom. Figure 9.7 shows the estimated hydrocarbon proven reserve holdings by company, underscoring the discrepancy between NOC versus IOC reserves. This suggests that an astonishing 90% of the world's known oil and gas reserves are being monopolized by NOCs. These figures likely underestimate the size of NOCs' oil reserves, as NOCs choose to keep the true size of their oil holdings opaque, and full geographic surveys may have missed further reserves.

Ironically, these NOCs arose amid a political backlash against Western imperialism, which supported once powerful companies such as the Anglo-Persian Oil Company or Standard Oil (the ancestors of today's IOCs) in developing indigenous resources in their colonies on financial terms extremely unfavorable to the weak host governments. The predatory behavior of these companies, which reaped the lion's share of revenue while giving only pittances to the local community, motivated a deep sense of political grievance. After many new resource-rich nation-states emerged out of the wreckage of European empires after World War II, "resource nationalism" came into vogue. The newly

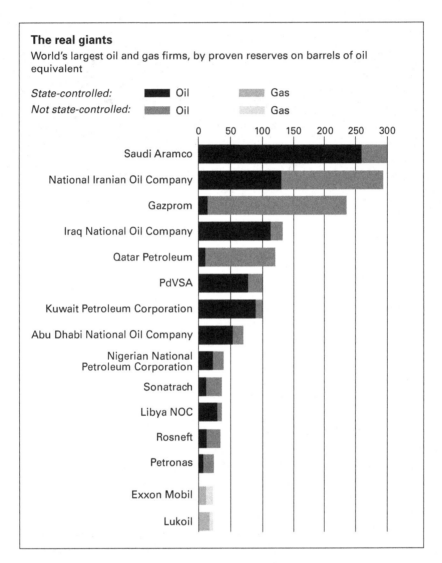

Figure 9.7
The real giants: world's largest oil and gas firms, by proven resources (in barrels of oil equivalent). National oil companies control 90% of the world's reserves.
Source: PFC Energy, reproduced in the *Economist* in 2006.

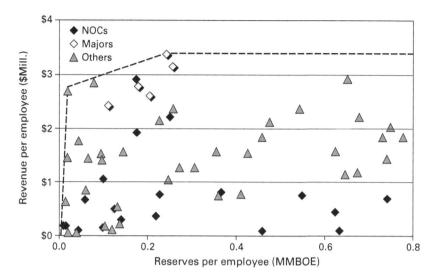

Figure 9.8
Operational efficiency of oil companies.

independent states formed NOCs to best utilize and preserve the value of mineral wealth for the local society and keep it out of the reach of predatory foreign companies.

Today the vast majority of the world's energy resources remain under the control of NOCs, which maintain a dual mandate of maximizing resource value and creating local jobs and funding welfare programs.

With a lack of competitive pressure because of their protected monopoly status and their dual mandate, it should be no surprise that NOCs have a dismal record of operational efficiency compared to their private counterparts. In 2007 the Baker Institute of Public Policy at Rice University produced a report that detailed the technical efficiency of oil companies by measuring the distance from an "efficient frontier" calculated in terms of revenue and reserves per employee, as seen in figures 9.8 and 9.9 (with 1.00 on the axis being at the efficient frontier, and lower numbers representing less efficiency).[1] NOCs were shown to be generally far less operationally efficient than IOCs at maximizing revenues, in light of the amount of reserves they possess.

1. Stacy L. Eller, Peter R. Hartley, and Kenneth B. Medlock III, "Empirical Evidence on the Operational Efficiency of National Oil Companies," *Empirical Economics* 40, no. 3 (2011): 623–643.

Moreover, the direct economic costs of this technical efficiency may pale in comparison with the indirect costs associated with a lack of access to reserves by competitive markets. It is difficult to accurately estimate this indirect cost as one must imagine a counterfactual world in which all oil reserves are subject to free and open competition and bidding.

But it is plausible that in this more liberal world, given the incredible concentration and bounty of proven hydrocarbon reserves in the Persian Gulf, where development costs are as low as $2 per barrel, the full power of modern technology and capital investment would have brought global oil prices in equilibrium to perhaps $10–$15 per barrel. Of course, because of the lack of access resulting from NOC monopolies, global oil prices have instead been in the $50–$100 range for the past few decades with short exceptions.

A simple back-of-the-envelope calculation suggests that a $40 price distortion in the global oil market amounts to an economic transfer from consumers to producers of $1.3 trillion annually. This distorted price in turn incentivizes private oil companies locked out of the most economical reserves to develop higher-cost sources, such as offshore, Arctic, and shale/tight unconventional oil. All those billions of dollars in global exploration and production may represent an economic distortion away from the economically ideal free-market equilibrium.

An intelligent observer from Mars may only shake its alien head at the collective folly of humanity as it sees us busily extracting and exhausting oil reserves in the most expensive, environmentally damaging, and technically most challenging areas of the Earth's crust, even as the easiest reserves remain underdeveloped. In a supreme irony, it is possible that in the future, the exhaustion of those hardest-to-reach oil reserves may spur the technological breakthroughs to alternative energy sources, making the oil in the most accessible and economical reserves obsolete, thanks to political distortions.

Commodity Producer Cartels

If the political distortions in the market for developing oil reserves (when the commodity is still underground) weren't enough, there are further political distortions affecting oil markets once the reserves have been developed and production capacity has been built.

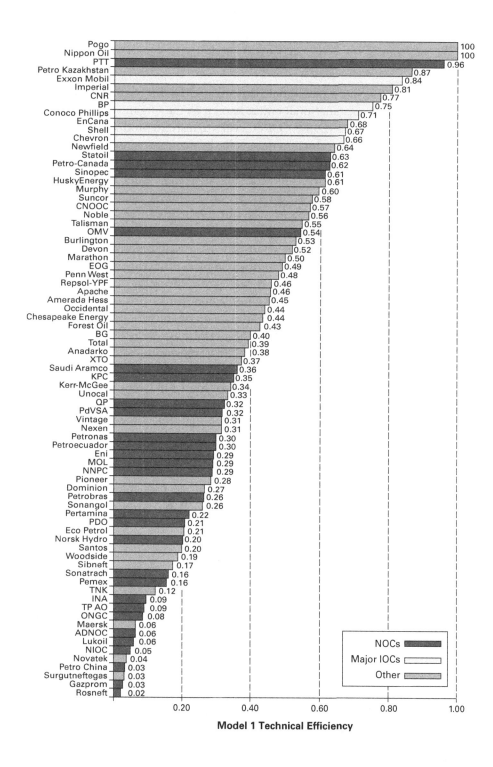

Figure 9.9
Distance to the efficient frontier. Output = revenue; inputs = gas reserves, oil reserves, employees.

Many of the same states that have created NOCs have also joined together into a supranational entity known as the Organization of Oil Producing Countries (OPEC). OPEC seeks to restrain production below capacity by setting production quotas for its member states to stabilize prices and extract further oligopolistic rents. While precise estimates are challenging to derive, the economic distortion from this explicit political manipulation of supply may still be much smaller than the indirect distortion stemming from lack of competitive access to develop the world's reserves and build production capacity in the first place.

However, OPEC is far from a perfectly monolithic organization, with geopolitical rivalries and the free-rider problem often causing its political unity to fall apart, as happened during the November 2014 meeting. With no rigorous mechanism of enforcement (unsurprising, given its supranational nature), production quotas set by the group can and are flouted by individual member states, ironically often by the same "hawks," such as Iran or Venezuela, that constantly call for tighter quotas (on others) and higher price targets (figure 9.10).

Saudi Arabia, as the largest and wealthiest holder of oil reserves with the economic and political will to maintain unused or spare production capacity, acts as the de facto leader of OPEC. It aspires to act as a "central bank" of oil, increasing or holding back output from its spare capacity, to bring price stability into markets (though at noncompetitive and elevated levels).

But this is notoriously challenging because of the naturally high volatility of oil prices, the inelasticity of demand and supply, the inabil-

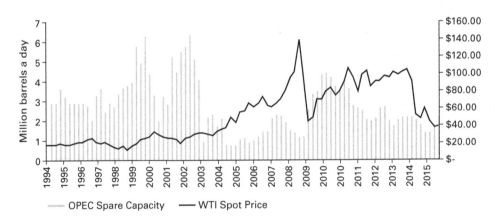

Figure 9.10
OPEC spare capacity vs. WTI spot prices.
Source: Bloomberg.

ity to immediately produce beyond installed capacity, the difficulties in coordinating politically with other producers (some of which, such as Russia or Iran, are geopolitical rivals), low transparency in both supply and demand, and surprises from non-OPEC production (such as the U.S. fracking revolution).

Nevertheless, to properly act as a "central bank," Saudi Arabia may wish to borrow from the playbook of modern central banks such as the U.S. Federal Reserve, which places immense emphasis on transparency to maintain its credibility and power to move markets. By contrast, the lack of transparency and openness in Saudi Arabia's energy sector leaves the window open for investor disbelief. This notably occurred in 2008 when oil prices were skyrocketing to $150/bbl. In an attempt to temper the oil price, Saudi Arabia announced the emergency additional production of 400 kb/d at an extraordinary meeting in Jeddah. Yet markets shrugged off this announcement, believing that Saudi Arabia lacked the production or reserve capacity to actually bring this additional supply to market. Ironically, by the time this production indeed came online, the bankruptcy of Lehman Brothers had triggered the global recession and subsequent financial crisis, and oil prices had plummeted. In turn, the recent planned partial privatization of Saudi Aramco and the corporate transparency that accompanies a public listing mark a potentially revolutionary change.

Energy Subsidies

Political distortions of energy markets are by no means isolated to the supply side of the equation. Demand can also be distorted by programs to subsidize fuel prices below market levels, often by the very same producers that are distorting supply. The International Monetary Fund estimated the costs of these negative fuel taxes at about $480 billion per year in 2011 (figures 9.11 and 9.12).[2] By contrast, renewable energy subsidies, mainly from the governments of the advanced economies, amounted to $120 billion in 2014.[3]

The list of economic harms caused by this distortion is long. Fuel subsidies cause fiscal deficits, crowd out needed social spending in other areas, depress private investment in deploying more energy efficient technologies, and incentivize the wasteful use of energy.

2. Benedict J. Clements, David Coady, Stefania Fabrizio, Sanjeev Gupta, Trevor Serge Coleridge Alleyne, and Carlo A. Sdralevich. *Energy Subsidy Reform: Lessons and Implications* (International Monetary Fund, 2013).
3. *World Energy Outlook 2014* (Paris: International Energy Agency, 2014).

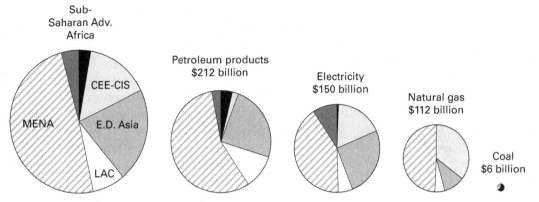

Figure 9.11
Share of total subsidies. Total pre-tax subsidies amounted to $480 billion in 2011.
Source: Benedict J. Clements, David Coady, Stefania Fabrizio, Sanjeev Gupta, Trevor
Serge Coleridge Alleyne, and Carlo A. Sdralevich, *Energy Subsidy Reform: Lessons and
Implications* (International Monetary Fund, 2013).

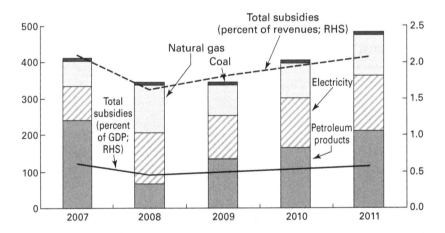

Figure 9.12
Total subsidies as a percent of revenues and GDP.
Sources: Staff estimates, Organisation for Economic Co-operation and Development,
International Energy Agency, Deutsche Gesellschaft für Internationale Zusammenarbeit,
the IMF's *World Economic Outlook*, and the World Bank. Data are based on most recent
year available. Total subsidies in percent of GDP and revenues are calculated as total
identified subsidies divided by global GDP and revenues, respectively. As reproduced
in Clements et al., *Energy Subsidy Reform*.

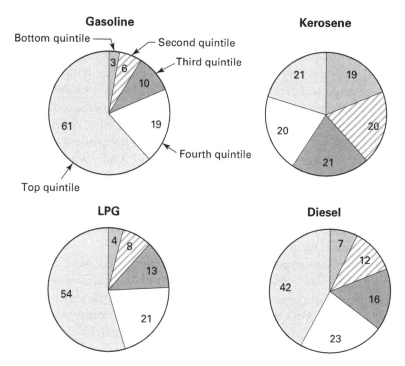

Figure 9.13
Distribution of fossil fuel subsidies to income groups by quintile.
Source: Arze del Granado, Francisco Javier, David Coady, and Robert Gillingham, "The Unequal Benefits of Fuel Subsidies: A Review of Evidence for Developing Countries," *World Development* 40, no. 11 (2012): 2234–2248.

Worse, even though subsidies are often justified as being a redistributive program for low-income households, they benefit the richest consumers the most (in absolute terms). The rich own and use cars and other energy-intensive equipment more extensively than the poor do. Figure 9.13 shows how 61% of the economic cost of gasoline fuel prices goes to the richest 20% of the income distribution. Yet paradoxically, in relative terms, subsidies form a larger share of the effective income of the poorest consumers, and doing away with fuel subsidies would hurt the poor more than the rich in relative terms.

However, with the fall in oil prices since 2014, many countries are making progress toward reducing energy subsidies. Exporter nations face pressures on their budgets, while importing nations can phase out subsidies and consumers still face still historically moderate market prices for oil.

Pipeline Geopolitics

Finally, some unique political distortions occur in natural gas markets. Unlike oil, which is liquid and thus easily transportable, natural gas is gaseous at room temperature. Transportation therefore requires either compression or cooling into liquid form or the construction of dedicated pipelines, both of which are costly. This is why natural gas markets, unlike oil or coal markets, are not yet globally integrated but are balkanized into various market pockets with their own idiosyncratic price dynamics.

Figure 9.14 compares the relative transport costs of shipborne oil and coal, oil and gas pipelines, and liquefied natural gas (LNG). At intermediate distances of 5,000 kilometers or less, pipelines represent the most economical form of transportation.

But pipelines are expensive to build, and operators of existing pipelines form "natural monopolies" as a result of the barriers to entry faced by potential competitors. Furthermore, gas pipelines are fixed assets that often cross national borders. Therefore, countries whose territories the pipeline transits also possess the ability to block the flow of gas through the pipeline.

This creates what economists call a "hold-up" problem, in which two or more actors must cooperate to create economic value but con-

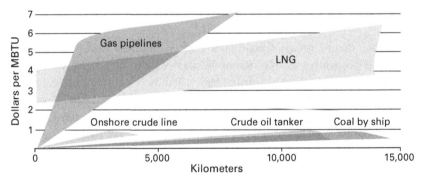

Note: The main determinants of gas transportation costs within the ranges indicated are: for pipelines, the diameter of the pipe and the terrain to be crossed; and for LNG, the initial costs of liquefaction capacity.

Figure 9.14
Indicative comparison of fossil fuel transportation costs. The main determinants of gas transportation costs within the ranges indicated are for gas pipelines, the diameter of the pipe and the terrain to be covered, and for LNG, the initial costs of liquefaction capacity.
Source: Adapted from Jensen Associates, reproduced by the International Energy Agency.

Figure 9.15
Eurasian pipelines.
Source: U.S. Energy Information Administration, 2009.

tracts between them are nonenforceable. Then any actor may have the incentive to "hold up" the project and destroy its value to increase its bargaining power and win a greater share of the revenue.

Nowhere is this problem more evident than in the natural gas pipelines crisscrossing the Eurasian landmass, notably those linking Russia to Western Europe (figure 9.15). Many of these pipelines were originally built by the former Soviet Union to send the natural gas from its western Siberian fields to its population centers in the western USSR and beyond, to gas-hungry customers in Germany and other parts of Western Europe. While the Soviet Union existed, there was no political distortion to impede the smooth flow of gas, at least in Soviet territory. But with the collapse of the Soviet Union and the emergence of independent states such as Belarus and Ukraine through whose sovereign territory these pipelines transited, the situation was ripe for the hold-up problem to emerge.

For example, after signing an agreement to supply natural gas at a certain price to customers in Germany, Russia's state gas monopoly, Gazprom, may be tempted to renege on the contract and hold out for better rates. From Germany's perspective, it may be better to capitulate than see its gas supplies interrupted. Or Ukraine might halt the flow of gas through its territory to bargain for higher transit fees or lower prices on its own gas.

The headaches around gas security have forced countries in Western Europe to search for more reliable alternatives and build resiliency into their natural gas supply system, including through the construction of regasification terminals for imported LNG and more storage and inter-connecting pipelines. In turn, Russia has poured billions of dollars into developing alternative pipelines that bypass problematic transit countries like Ukraine, such as the Nord Stream under the Baltic Sea or the planned South Stream pipeline under the Black Sea. These moves in turn have angered the United States, which is concerned by the improving bargaining power of Russia relative to Ukraine's and the increasing vulnerability of U.S. allies in Western Europe to further energy blackmail by Russia.

All of these additional pipelines and infrastructure are not the ideal outcome, as expanding existing pipelines would have been far more economical. They exist only because of the peculiarities of natural gas markets. But until a mechanism can be found to enforce natural gas contracts between sovereign entities and minimize the hold-up problem, such political distortions are likely to continue.

10 Commodity Markets and Financial Regulation

In this chapter, we return to some of the issues raised in earlier chapters about the proper role of regulation in improving the market efficiency of financial markets for commodities.[1] We have already discussed the various reasons for participating in such financial activities as hedging, speculation, and portfolio investment. Ideally, these financial markets serve consumers and producers in managing their commodity price risk effectively and aid in economic decision making.

But the dizzying rally in global commodity prices in 2007 followed by their crash in 2008 added to skepticism over the proper regulation of commodity markets. First, as oil prices rose to a record high of $147.47/bbl in July 2007, many policy makers blamed the record amount of financial investment in commodities, notably by passive index investors, for the record-high prices. Warren Buffett famously dubbed derivatives the financial equivalent of weapons of mass destruction.

Subsequently, the onset of the worst global economic and financial crisis in a century, triggered by the bankruptcy of Lehman Brothers in September 2008, gave further impetus to regulatory efforts. Governments around the world stepped in to bail out troubled financial institutions, while regulators initiated a suite of reforms, such as the Dodd-Frank Act of 2010 and the Third Basel Accord, to tame unruly financial markets.

We have also discussed the various imperfections in commodity financial markets that make them prone to behavioral anomalies despite the discounting of many experts. To recap, first, the demand for and the supply of many commodities are highly price inelastic and nonlinear. This is because a large supply or demand response requires

---

1. The following section on regulation of commodity trading draws substantively from Daniel P. Ahn, "Improving Energy Market Regulation" (Council on Foreign Relations, February 1, 2011) (http://www.jstor.org/stable/resrep00275).

high upfront fixed costs from producers and consumers (e.g., to open a new producing basin or upgrade the efficiency of equipment). In turn, even the slightest excess demand or supply would trigger violent price responses, making it difficult for market participants to formulate price expectations.

This situation, where there is naturally high volatility, is further worsened by the fact that commodity markets are notoriously opaque. As we saw earlier, the clear majority of proven reserves of crude oil and natural gas are kept by nontransparent national oil companies (NOCs), which divulge little information about their reserves. There are simply no credible data available for key aspects of the fundamental balance, such as the amount of Saudi spare capacity or the size of Chinese inventories.

The lack of insight into economic fundamentals forces information-starved market participants to copy the behavior of others, leading to herd behavior. The shortage of information also leads market observers to focus inordinately on the handful of available signals, such as weekly changes in U.S. inventories, even if they are misleading signals of the overall state of global demand or supply.

And the paucity of reliable information can lend dangerous plausibility to some of the wilder narratives on commodity fundamentals (e.g., peak oil). And despite the idealistic hopes of economists that any mispricings should quickly be arbitraged away, the inelasticity of supply and demand may prevent the visible physical response necessary to persuade market participants otherwise. The traditional mechanisms that would cause prices to return to true equilibrium levels, namely, efficient absorption of information and physical adjustment of markets, can be weak in the short term. Furthermore, speculative behavior can further exacerbate this unnatural volatility, especially if it drives the mispricing in a single direction, resulting in the formation of asset bubbles.

Bubbles typically begin with some plausible if ill-understood theory behind the increasing fundamental value behind some asset or commodity. For instance, uncertainty around the internet revolution led to the dot-com bubble, which burst in 2001, and the Dutch tulip bulb mania in 1637. New "speculative" demand linked to prices enters the market, with investors seeking to sell to the "bigger fool" rather than assess the true equilibrium value of the commodity.

Eventually, of course, economic reality sets in and the excess supply in the good or commodity is finally recognized, resulting in the rapid collapse of prices and the destruction of trend-following speculative demand. But in the meantime, this volatility can cause massive damage to the economy through the collapse of systemically important financial institutions and the ruin of many retail investors unlucky enough to be caught up in the speculative frenzy. If the bubble occurs in sensitive "staple" goods like food or energy, the political temperature can rise quickly.

Politicians often like to ask sophistic questions, such as "Does speculation drives prices?" This is as meaningless as the question, "Does law cause crime?" On the one hand, at a tautological level, law does "cause" crime as without laws, there would be no such thing as a crime. Similarly, speculation naturally drives prices as traders transmit the information into market prices through the very act of trading. This is simply part of the mechanical process of buying and selling in any well-functioning market. But a more meaningful question to ask is, "How should one design/regulate markets to improve price discovery and minimize unnatural (if inevitable) deviations away from true equilibrium prices?" Despite Conant's defense of speculation, he too understood and cautioned against uninformed speculators who could distort prices temporarily.

Rather than ideologically railing against speculation in general, regulators should consider policies that would nudge the obvious imperfections of commodity markets closer to the classical ideal of Charles Conant. These policies include regulations to ensure the following:

1. Good information entering into the fundamentals of demand and supply.
2. Freedom and willingness on the part of traders who do possess information to enter markets and transmit said information efficiently into prices.
3. Good market design to prevent market manipulation, rent-seeking, and financial illiquidity and systemic risk contagion.

Commodity Market Regulation in the United States

In response to the global recession of 2008–2009, the U.S. Congress passed the Dodd-Frank Wall Street Reform and Consumer Protection Act of 2010, the most comprehensive regulatory overhaul of financial markets since the Great Depression. In commodity markets, the Dodd-Frank Act mandated changes in four key areas:

1. **Transparency**, including disaggregated position reporting, large trade reporting, and real-time reporting of trade information in a data depository.
2. **Centralized clearing** of standardized swap contracts through a centralized counterparty clearinghouse.
3. **Higher capital and margin requirements**, especially for bilateral OTC swaps, following Basel III rules.
4. **Position limits** that limit the maximum size of trade positions in certain commodities by noncommercial participants, that is, "speculators."

Let us discuss these four aspects of the Dodd-Frank Act in greater detail.

Physical Transparency

As discussed earlier, commodity markets inevitably feature large and unavoidable price swings. Forcibly suppressing them would only harm the efficient functioning of markets. Yet this does not mean that all price swings are fundamentally justified or desirable. The textbook role of a market price is to adjust to find the appropriate price level to equalize required demand for an economic good with available supply. The most basic ingredient for stable and efficient price discovery is public and credible information on the sources of demand and supply.

The current state of transparency in the many commodity markets, however, is decrepit. Here we may take the example of oil markets. Only a handful of advanced economies in the Organisation for Economic Co-operation and Development (OECD) provide any timely statistical releases on their oil demand-and-supply balances through their membership in the International Energy Agency (IEA). At the time of the IEA's founding in 1974, OECD member countries accounted for almost three quarters of global oil demand. Today they account for less than half of the world's oil consumption, and their share continues to fall quickly. Total world oil demand is projected to grow from roughly 90 million barrels per day at present to over 100 million barrels a day by 2035. But nearly all of that incremental increase is projected to come from non-OECD member states (e.g., China, India), where transparency is much poorer, decreasing the OECD's share to only a third of global consumption by 2035 (figure 10.1).

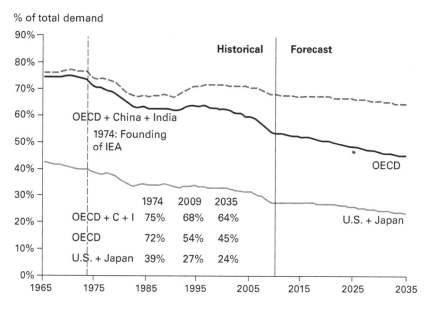

Figure 10.1
OECD share in global oil demand compared to other participants' share. The OECD was
founded in 1974.
Source: BP, U.S. Energy Information Administration.

Data on the supply side of the equation are similarly poor, with
OECD member countries accounting for less than one quarter of the
world's crude oil production. Market production share is dominated
by the Organization of Petroleum Exporting Countries (OPEC) and the
states of the former Soviet Union, none of which is particularly trans-
parent. Together, they account for over half of world production. Even
worse, while world oil demand is aggregated from the decentralized
needs of millions of individual consumers, and therefore has at least
some relationship to economic growth, production from OPEC and the
former Soviet states has often been subject to the political calculations
of NOCs.

Despite significant efforts to enhance the transparency of demand
and supply statistics through such laudable initiatives as the Joint Oil
Data Initiative (JODI), there is much room for improvement. Participa-
tion in JODI is purely voluntary, and there is no penalty for omitting
or refusing to submit data. Further, the data submissions are not subject
to third-party review or public scrutiny of the collection processes,
leading to questions over the credibility and accuracy of the data.

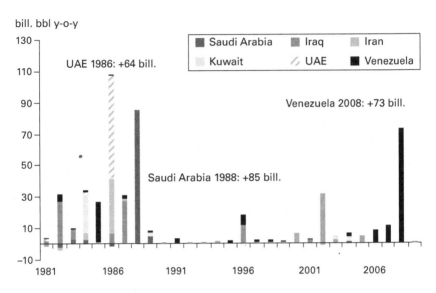

Figure 10.2
OPEC members' year-by-year revisions to official proven reserves.
Source: BP, U.S. Energy Information Administration.

Members of OPEC, who operate an imperfect oligopoly and receive official production quotas proportional to estimated official reserves, can and are sorely tempted to fudge official production reports when politically expedient. For example, in 1984 Kuwait abruptly raised its official proven reserves from 67 billion barrels to 93 billion barrels. Other nations, such as Saudi Arabia, the United Arab Emirates, and Iran, determined to maintain their own quota levels, followed suit. Figure 10.2 shows how key OPEC members have been manipulating their reserves statistics over the years in a bid to capture more production quotas. Nor is this behavior a thing of the past. As recently as 2008, Venezuela revised its official reserve levels upward by an astonishing 73 billion barrels.

Most mature financial markets have—after the hard lessons of numerous panics and accounting shortfalls—made a point to provide full, timely, and accurate accounting disclosures that are publicly available. An investor in U.S. equity markets, for example, may, when formulating a fair price, freely look up the cash flow, assets, and liabilities of a company by reviewing the company's filings with the U.S. Securities and Exchange Commission. Energy market traders have no such recourse. Instead, they must extrapolate from incomplete, infrequent, and often inaccurate data to make intelligent guesses of the appropriate equilibrium price level.[2]

In an ideal world, the U.S. government could fix this problem by mandating physical transparency requirements of all companies that produce or consume oil traded on U.S. markets, just as it requires transparency from companies that are publicly traded in the United States. Yet this faces a fundamental problem: the prices of U.S.-traded oil contracts depend on the global balance between oil demand and supply, but the United States lacks the regulatory reach to require transparency on a global scale. Physical transparency in commodity markets is thus as much a foreign policy problem as it is a financial regulatory problem.

Financial Transparency

As with physical transparency, certain financial transparency initiatives hold great potential for improving market efficiency and deterring excessive risk taking and market manipulation. However, policy makers must also be alert to the real trade-offs inherent in substantial transparency initiatives and to the political opposition that will be engendered from the affected interests.

To achieve improved financial transparency, policymakers should improve the quality of statistical reporting and make statistics more accessible by creating a real-time data depository. On the statistical reporting front, the U.S. Commodities Futures Trading Commission (CFTC) has made important progress by providing new disaggregated Commitment of Traders (COT) reports on a weekly basis since September 2009. These new reports provide a finer decomposition of trader's holdings than previous reports, separating traders into the following four categories (Previously the CFTC used to classify market participants into "commercial" and "noncommercial" participants):

1. **Producer/Merchant/Processor/User**: An entity that predominantly engages in the production, processing, packing, or handling of a physical commodity and uses the futures markets to manage or hedge risks associated with those activities. Typical examples in the energy

2. The difference, of course, is not quite so stark. For example, equity prices in growth companies such as tech startups also feature difficult-to-quantify values, and even those markets with fairly good microlevel data such as housing markets also saw price overshooting in mortgage-backed securities.

space would be an oil producer, a refinery, an airline, or a pipeline operator.

2. **Swap dealer**: A "swap dealer" is an entity that deals primarily in swaps for a commodity and uses the futures markets to manage or hedge the risk associated with those swaps transactions. Typically, large investment banks play an important role as swap dealers managing commodity financial exposure for their clients, which can include traditional producer/users but also hedge funds and other financial speculators.

3. **Money manager**: A "money manager" is a registered commodity-trading advisor (CTA), a registered commodity pool operator (CPO), or an unregistered fund identified by CFTC. These traders are engaged in managing and conducting organized futures trading on behalf of clients. This class arguably comes closest to the "financial speculator" often mentioned in the press. But it is important to note that a large proportion of speculative positions, including those from institutional investors into commodity indices, is likely made through swap contacts and shows up in futures markets only through swap dealers.

4. **Other reportables**: Every other reportable trader that is not placed into one of the other three categories is placed into the "other reportables" category. It is disconcerting that this category are increasing in size lately.

For each category, the CFTC provides the amount of long, short, or in spread (offsetting long and short) positions (figure 10.3).

While a vast improvement from the previous classification of market participants simply into "commercial" and "noncommercial" categories, this system still exhibits considerable shortcomings. First, as the swap dealer category itself suggests, the COT reports cover only the futures market and not the vast and largely opaque OTC swaps market, which often trades "look-alike" contracts similar in function to standard futures contracts.

Second, the producer/merchant/processor/user and swap dealer classifications are still too broad. To take an example, an oil producer typically hedges by selling short some futures contracts to lock in a price for a set amount of sales. By contrast, an oil consumer, such as an airline, typically hedges by going long on futures contracts to lock in a price for a set amount of purchases. Together, a category that includes oil producers and consumers would see the natural short positions of

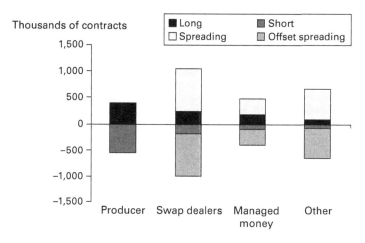

Figure 10.3
Sample positioning data of long, short, and spreading positions in a commodity futures market by investor category.
Source: CTFC.

producers and the natural long positions of consumers cancel each other out, making the net positions reported under this category difficult to interpret.

Similarly, the swap dealer category may wash-out many offsetting long and short positions held by the counterparties of the swap dealers. Ideally, reporting should be further disaggregated into producers, users, and processors, to prevent the washing out of natural long and short positions, while swap dealers should record and report those positions made on behalf of commercial operators, managed money investors, or other swap dealers.

The COT reports are also silent on the timing or "term structure" of market participants' financial exposure. For example, current reports cannot distinguish between money managers forming positions in short-term natural gas contracts in response to, say, expectations of a temporary heat wave versus positions formed in long-term natural gas contracts in response to expectations of increased demand from China. But this difference matters to market stability.

For example, Metallgesellschaft AG, an energy wholesaler, failed in 1993 because of the unsustainability of the term structure of its risk management strategy. The large size of its losses (roughly $1.5 billion in 1993 dollars) and the forced liquidation of its massive positions caused systemic tremors throughout the financial system. This underscores the need for regulators to have a clear understanding of the term structure of aggregate commodity risk held by financial participants.

Real-Time Data Depository

In addition to improving the quality of statistical reporting, the CFTC also now mandates the creation of real-time post-trade swap data repositories (SDRs) to publicly report the date, time, trade size, price, and counterparty identities moments after every swap transaction. Not only does this shed reporting light on opaque markets and alert regulators of potentially dangerous risk-taking behavior but a real-time data repository promises to reduce price volatility by anchoring prices to the terms of previous transactions.

For example, any sensible customer would likely refuse to buy a crude oil contract at a price very different from $20 a barrel when she knows that literally moments earlier a customer before her paid precisely that. Furthermore, a real-time data repository would lower the customer's costs of executing commodity financial transactions, potentially allowing more cost-effective risk management by physical companies wishing to hedge commercial risk or retail investors seeking exposure.

Such an initiative is not new for the financial industry. The Trade Reporting and Compliance Engine (TRACE), which was introduced into the corporate bond market in 2002 by the U.S.-based Financial Industry Regulatory Authority (FINRA), provided a natural experiment for financial economists to study the impact of such transparency on liquidity and market efficiency. Multiple studies have found that TRACE has improved liquidity, but only in the narrow sense of reducing trade execution costs. Market liquidity, a term often used loosely by policy makers, can mean multiple things. It may mean the degree of market "tightness," or the cost required to execute a transaction immediately, generally measured by the spread between the offer price faced by a buyer and the bid price faced by a seller. But liquidity can also mean depth, the ability of markets to absorb large buy and sell orders with minimum impact on prices, or resiliency, the speed with which market prices recover from an unexpected order.

According to TRACE's example, a real-time post-trade data repository for commodity OTC contracts will significantly reduce market tightness, or the average execution cost faced by a customer. This also means that market makers, who reap the spreads between bid and ask prices, will lose the economic rent they extract from less informed customers. However, there are longer-term trade-offs that must be considered. By reducing the option value of holding contracts in the prospect of closing a trade, real-time reporting disincentivizes dealers from holding inventory to execute large trades. Thus liquidity gains in reducing market tightness may be offset by losses in market depth.

Centralized Clearing

The 2008 financial crisis focused a spotlight on the interconnected web of bilateral credit relationships among the large systemically important financial institutions that helped propagate the initial shock of the failure of Lehman Brothers into a catastrophic systemwide loss of liquidity.

A central counterparty clearing (CCP) mechanism promises to stem financial contagion, by imposing, as the name implies, a central counterparty between the original transacting parties to guarantee execution of the transaction. Appropriately, the Dodd-Frank Act of 2010 emphasizes the mandatory trading of standardized OTC swaps through CCP clearing houses. Financial participants can make transactions confident that they are protected from idiosyncratic counterparty risk by the creditworthiness of the CCP. Furthermore, introducing transparency, record-keeping, and risk supervision is more logistically straightforward for a CCP clearing house than for the often dense and impenetrable records of multiple bilateral transactions.

However, a CCP clearing house requires economies of scale to be efficient, liquid, and cost-effective, and CCP clearing carries risks as well. In effect, a CCP clearing house consolidates the risks of multiple bilateral credit relationships into one giant centralized risk deposit, effectively aggregating multiple medium-sized risks into one extreme "too-big-to-fail" entity, namely, the house itself. In a system of bilateral arrangements (the left-hand side of figure 10.4), the failure of one firm (A) leads to losses for other firms (B, C) that contract with it. Contagion arises when one of the counterparties—say, firm B—begins to question firm C's exposure to firm A's failures and by extension, firm C's ability to remain solvent as its counterparty to the set of bilateral agreements it has with firm C. This shroud of uncertainty leads to a rapid drying up of liquidity in markets, creating significant rollover risk for firms that are highly leveraged with short-term liabilities, particularly when they have nothing to post for margin calls. The CCP system (the right-hand

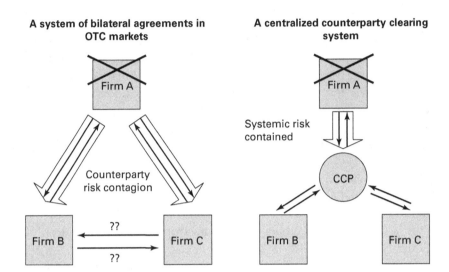

Figure 10.4
Contrasting risk-sharing in a system of bilateral arrangements versus a central counter-party

side of figure 10.4) reduces this risk by bringing all parties to the table, netting exposures, and guaranteeing execution of transactions.

Theoretically, private insurance may be sufficient to manage house systemic risk, given its greater transparency and ease of quantification compared to the nontransparent bank balance sheet risks without mark-to-market procedures. But taxpayers may again be liable if a critical CCP house becomes vulnerable as a result of the failure of several of its constituent members and insurers because of other outside risks.

Furthermore, the network effects of such consolidation are still poorly understood. Preliminary studies suggest that aggregate credit risk would be reduced only when multiple different derivative classes, such as commodities, foreign exchange, and credit-default swaps, are jointly cleared in a single CCP rather than separately cleared through two or more CCPs.[3] This again suggests that international coordination between regulators will be helpful to ensure that sufficient economies of scale are achieved with a minimum number of CCP clearinghouses.

3. Darrell Duffie and Haoxiang Zhu, "Does a Central Clearing Counterparty Reduce Counterparty Risk?," Stanford University Graduate School of Business Research Paper 2022 (July 2010), shows how for plausible scenarios, creating a CCP for a single class of derivatives would reduce netting efficiency and increase average default exposure.

However, this raises difficult questions as to whether the U.S. government, and ultimately taxpayers, would become liable if, for instance, a Europe-based CCP clearinghouse heavily used by U.S. financial institutions failed. Indeed, this is just one instance of a broader question confronting any systemically important part of the postcrisis global financial architecture: if it fails, which nation, if any, would be responsible for footing the bill of a rescue?

Beyond the issue of responsibility, would any electorate or government accept a solution that might see power or control of a systemically important financial institution ceded to a foreign or supranational entity?

As such, the feasibility of the CCP solution goes beyond economics itself. Regulatory harmonization and cooperation between the various national regulators is indispensable to prevent a tragedy of the commons whereby each nation wishes to defer the regulatory and financial burdens of managing systemic risk to others. Figure 10.5 shows how the mandating of CCP may be shifting the probability of financial crises further along the tail, lowering the probability of

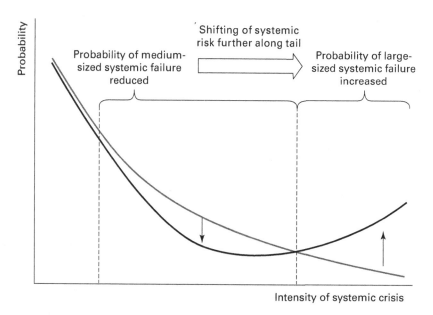

Figure 10.5
Probability of transfer of systemic risk.

moderately intense financial crises but raising the probability of very extreme ones.

Capital and Margins Requirements

In the aftermath of the global financial crisis of 2008–2009, one of the immediate regulatory responses was to require banks and other financial institutions to meet more stringent capital and liquidity requirements. Certainly, regulatory capital can be a powerful tool in curbing excessive risk-taking and preventing systemic crises, and both the U.S. Federal Reserve and other financial policy-making houses use capital and margin requirements and financial stress-tests to enhance macroprudential supervision.

However, unlike transparency and centralized clearing requirements, which has promising gains in market efficiency and improved systemic risk control, the effects of capital and margin requirements on market efficiency are more ambiguous. Setting capital requirements proportionate to the amount of risk a party assumes is more an art than a science.

On one hand, in the context of OTC markets, regulators appear determined to impose stricter capital and margin requirements on non-centrally cleared derivative transactions, given the greater potential counterparty risks of bilateral relationships over a CCP. This may additionally incentivize financial participants to use more exchange-traded and CCP-cleared standardized transactions, creating the desirable economies of scale discussed earlier.

On the other hand, high capital and margin requirements might unnecessarily weaken the legitimate market for customized OTC products. The additional amount of cash or equivalent that must be posted as a collateral for margin calls might be significant enough to deter the formation of such idiosyncratic markets to begin with. For instance, a contract linked to a non-benchmark grade of jet fuel might be of great importance to jetliners but excessively stringent regulatory requirements for OTC products might destroy the market, leading to the loss of a potential hedging instrument.

In addition, it is important to note that stricter requirements may not necessarily reduce financial volatility but may even contribute to it after the fact. Again, regulators may draw lessons from the 1993 failure of Metallgesellshaft AG, a large energy wholesaler. Metallgesellshaft AG had offered long-term (five- to ten-year) contracts promising delivery of heating oil and gasoline at fixed prices to retailers, and offset these obligations through the purchases of near-term futures contracts. This risk management strategy proved unviable when the term structure of energy prices moved into contango, in which short-term prices drop below long-term prices. Putting aside the wisdom of such risk management practices in principle, the deterioration of their marked-to-market short-term futures positions triggered a cascade of margin calls that eventually led to collapse and a systemwide loss of confidence, even when Metallgesellshaft AG may have been technically solvent with its promised future cash flows.

Given the extreme volatility and the significant possibility of large swings in commodity prices relative to the prices of other financial products, overly onerous margin requirements may result in a far higher frequency of the margin calls that trigger the sorts of systemic failures that the requirements try to prevent in the first place. In other words, tighter margin requirements may reduce some risk-taking in the first place, but once a contract is written, every amount of risk taken ultimately increases the chance of a margin-call driven forced liquidation. This leaves the overall impact on systemic risk uncertain.

Position Limits and Hedge Exemptions

If there is legitimate concern about whether higher capital and margin requirements can ultimately improve market efficiency, the author finds the efficacy of position limits even more ambiguous. Politicians have found something timelessly appealing in the idea that somehow manually capping the presence of speculators can prevent the next bubble and reduce market volatility. Not only does this ignore the gaping shortfalls in physical and financial transparency that may better address market volatility, it also ignores the irreversible growth of financial derivatives linked to commodities. Binding position limits will likely be counterproductive in restraining excessive speculation and may be useful only for the narrower purpose of preventing market manipulation. There are several reasons why position limits or hedging exemptions have limited effect on reining in excessive speculative behavior.

First of all, enforcing position limits will draw regulatory resources away from other responsibilities and add cumbersome regulatory regimes to the often ill-defined boundaries between exempt commercial hedging and speculative risk taking. Enforcement is further hampered by the fact that market participants will still be able to create alternative offshore investor entities and vehicles in other financial centers such as Dubai, Shanghai, or Singapore. Given the logistic challenges of enforcing tight position limits, regulators would be better advised to first address shortfalls in physical and financial transparency before turning to more radical interventions.

In the United States., the Commodity Exchanges Act grants the CFTC the authority to impose limits on the size of speculative positions in the futures market. Today, twenty-eight key commodities or "Core Referenced Futures Contracts," ranging from agricultural contracts to the four energy contracts on NYMEX are subjected to set of position limits depending on whether the contract is within the month of delivery and without ("spot month" vs. "non-spot month"). Although spot-month limits have been around prior to the Dodd-Frank legislation, the newly added non-spot month was subjected to greater public scrutiny.

In recognition that there is a genuine need for hedging by commercial entities, the CFTC also grant exemptions to bona fide commercial hedgers with physical exposure and swaps dealers qualifying under a newly created financial "risk management" exemption. While commercial hedgers are permitted to take up positions of unlimited size, swap dealers only receive a "partial exemption" as limited to two times the position limit (on a single-month or all-months-combined basis). Although the CFTC has rightly declined to offer exemptions to index funds and ETFs, the regulation has had an unintended effect of pushing fund managers to turn to OTC swaps to meet their new position limits, effectively transferring risk from one segment of the financial market to another, since investors in these funds now face counterparty risks.

Conclusion

The preceding sections have highlighted the need for measured caution and sensitivity when regulating commodity financial markets. Commodity prices will unavoidably continue to fluctuate intensely given fundamentally low elasticities of demand and supply, making full price management impossible. The key is to recognize the fact that there is natural volatility in commodity markets due to imperfect information. As such, policymakers should not be obsessed with stamping out on all speculative behavior, but rather design policies that reduce unnecessary market volatility and align market prices closer to fair valuations. Both blanket hostility toward speculative activity and unbridled faith in deregulated markets preclude intelligent efforts to improve markets.

11 Electricity Markets

In this chapter we cover some the most salient aspects of the economics of electricity markets, focusing on the peculiarities of the U.S. power system. Unlike most of the commodities we have discussed thus far, electricity is unique in that it is not a static physical good but rather a "state" of relative electron excitation or energy potential difference. By maintaining this potential difference, one can create a flow of negatively charged electrons, or an electric current. This can be harnessed for useful work, such as being converted into mechanical energy by an electric motor or used to generate visible light by running the current through the filament of a light bulb.

As it is not a physical good, it is quite expensive to "store" electricity. Despite recent strides in battery and other power storage technologies, electricity supply must still largely adjust in real time to fluctuations in demand. When electricity is generated, one cannot simply "put it aside" and use it tomorrow as one might a hunk of iron ore or a barrel of oil.

Furthermore, any generated power cannot be directly ascribed to a particular supplier. Because of their quantum nature, electrons are physically indistinguishable. Once it's in the grid, it's in the grid, so to speak. Also, the laws of physics dictate that the electrons always flow to the lowest-potential energy gradient (subject, of course, to capacity constraints, physical resistivity, etc.) no matter the desires of economic incentives or government fiat.

These special physical characteristics make electricity markets unlike the other commodity markets hitherto studied, and both economists and regulators have had to adapt their systems and methodological approaches to suit the peculiar characteristics of power. In a colloquial sense, "electricity" and "power" are often used interchangeably, as we shall in the remainder of this chapter, but power has a specific physical

Table 11.1
Some Common Physical Concepts in Electricity

Concept	Definition	Letter	Mathematical Relationship to Others	Common Units of Measurement
Electric charge	A fundamental physical property of matter that causes it to experience electromagnetic force, one of the four fundamental forces of nature	q		Coulomb (C)
Electric work	The amount of energy used to displace electric charges through the application of electric force	W		Joules (J), British Thermal Units (BTU), Kilowatt-Hours (KWh)
Voltage	The difference in electric potential between two points, or the electric work done per unit of electric charge	V	$= W/Q$	Volts (V)
Electric current	The rate of the flow of electric charge per unit of time	I	$= Q/t$	Amperes (A)
Power	The amount of electric work done per unit of time	P	$= W/t$	Watts (W)
Electric resistance	A measure of the difficulty with which an electric current passes through a conductor	R	$= V/I$	Ohm (Ω)
Capacitance	The ability of a body to store electric charge	C	$= q/V$	Farad (F)

meaning as well. Table 11.1 summarizes some of the most common physical concepts in electricity markets.

The Structure of Power Markets

The delivery system for power can be broken down into three main components: generation, transmission, and distribution (figure 11.1).

Generation
The generation sector refers to the power plants and stations that naturally generate the power. Many modern power plants, such as coal, natural gas, oil, nuclear, or hydropower stations, use water or super-heated steam to spin turbines and convert the mechanical energy into

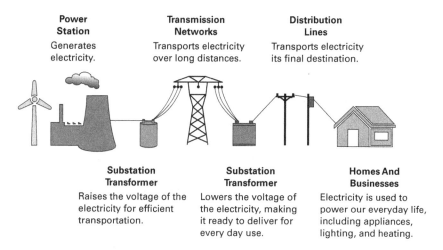

Power Station
Generates electricity.

Transmission Networks
Transports electricity over long distances.

Distribution Lines
Transports electricity its final destination.

Substation Transformer
Raises the voltage of the electricity for efficient transportation.

Substation Transformer
Lowers the voltage of the electricity, making it ready to deliver for every day use.

Homes And Businesses
Electricity is used to power our everyday life, including appliances, lighting, and heating.

Figure 11.1
Three components of power delivery: generation, transport, and distribution.
Source: Australian Energy Regulator.

electrical energy. But most solar power plants use photovoltaic cells to directly convert the solar energy from sunlight into an electric current.

Figure 11.2 shows the breakdown and outlook for U.S. power generation by fuel type to 2040. Natural gas is rapidly gaining market share, followed by renewable sources such as solar and wind, at the expense of coal and nuclear power. However, differences in their costs and intermittency mean these sources of power are not perfect substitutes but can complement each other as base versus peaking power sources in an electric grid.

In the United States, generation capacity may be operated by publicly owned utilities and private utilities such as independent power producers (IPP), and regulated by state-level utility commissions.

Transmission

The transmission sector is responsible for transporting the power over long distances from the generating station to the final area of distribution and consumption. The power is typically passed first through a transformer to raise the voltage of the power to reduce transmission losses before being transformed back to a lower voltage for local distribution.

In the United States, once power transmission lines cross state boundaries, transmission is regulated by the Federal Energy Regulatory

Trillion kilowatthours

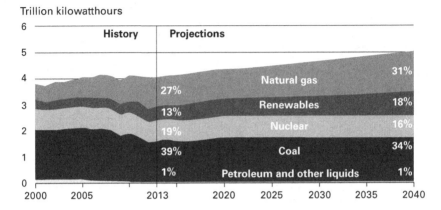

Figure 11.2
U.S. electricity generation by source, 2000–2040 (AEO2015 reference case).
Source: U.S. Energy Information Administration.

Commission (FERC), which has divided the continental United States into transmission planning regions, with the notable exception of parts of Texas, which operate under an entirely independent system operator (ISO) known as the Electric Reliability Council of Texas (ERCOT) (figure 11.3). We return to the topic of ISOs later.

Distribution
The final component of the delivery system for power is the distribution sector, which distributes the power at lower voltage to retail consumers. In the United States, local distribution is at 120 volts (for lighting and other wall sockets) or 240 volts (for large appliances).

Traditional versus Deregulated Ownership Structures

In the traditional structure of ownership, a single utility (often a state-owned utility) owns all levels of the power delivery system, from the generators and substations to the transmission and distribution lines (figure 11.4). This vertical integration makes operation and regulation simple, with a single owner incentivized to streamline the entire integrated delivery system from top to bottom. If the utility is state-owned, then, at least in theory, its goals are aligned with the optimal welfare of society.

However, this structure can bring its own problems, as the lack of competition and the monopolistic status of many vertically integrated

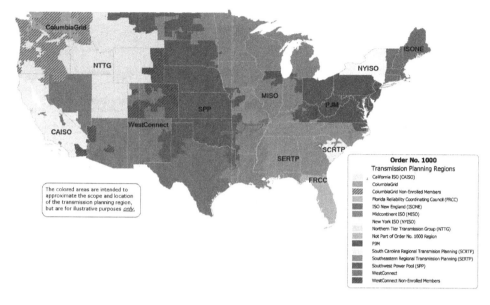

Figure 11.3
FERC transmission planning regions under order 1000.

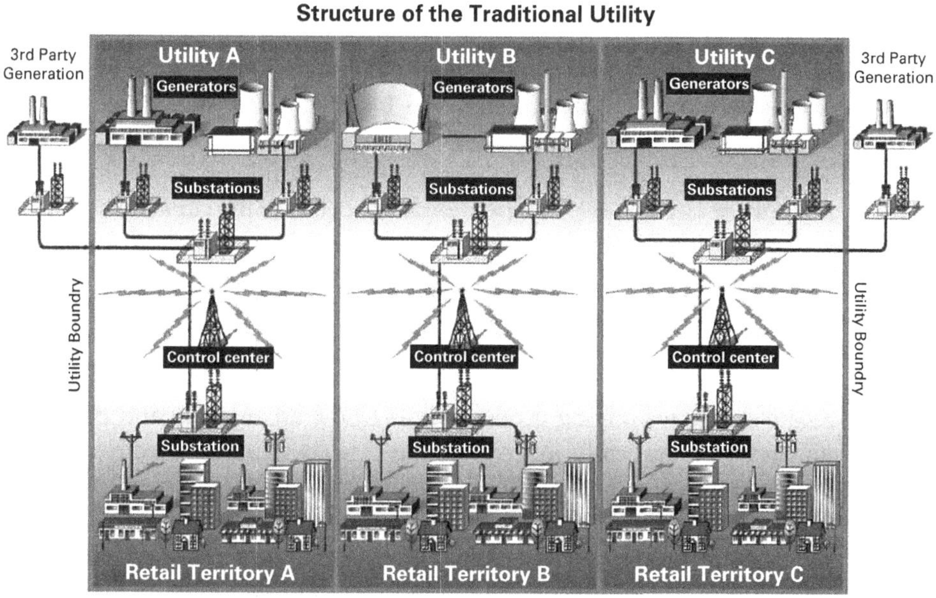

Structure of the Traditional Utility

Figure 11.4
Ownership structure of traditional vertically integrated utilities.

Structure of the Deregulated Electric Supply System

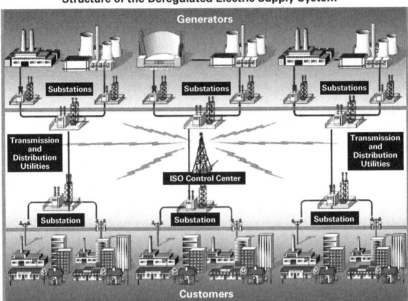

Figure 11.5
Ownership structure of deregulated electricity supply systems.

utilities can breed their own inefficiencies. In many advanced economies, electricity market deregulation has broken this vertical integration. In the generation sector, both traditional public utilities and
private generators (e.g., IPPs) compete directly in power auctions to
supply power. There is also competition in markets for the capacity and
forward provision of power.

But the transmission and distribution sectors remain coordinated
under regional transmission operators (RTOs) or ISOs to ensure the
efficient allocation and pricing for electricity in the RTO's area of
responsibility (figure 11.5).

Debate continues among economists as to the advantages and dis-
advantages of a vertically integrated versus a deregulated electricity
system. In the United States, the electricity crisis in 2000 in the West,
chiefly California, still attracts controversy, with some arguing that
failures in system design and incentivization caused the crisis and
others pointing to market manipulation by predatory companies like
Enron.

A full discussion of the economics of electricity sector deregulation is beyond the scope of this book. But based on the experiences of the United States and other economies that have deregulated electricity, such as the United Kingdom, it appears that deregulation is hard to do right. If done properly and in full, however, it can produce significant economic benefits in terms of reducing monopolistic power and bringing greater competition and transparency in the industry and, ultimately, lower retail prices for consumers.

Electricity Demand and Supply: Load Duration, Price Dispatch, and Price Duration Curves

Now we turn to the mechanics of electricity demand and supply. To properly describe power demand, we must consider the demand profile at very high frequencies since demand load fluctuates continuously throughout the day owing to demand factors such as temperature fluctuations and the day/night cycle. Figure 11.6 shows how power demand is low during the night hours when people are asleep.

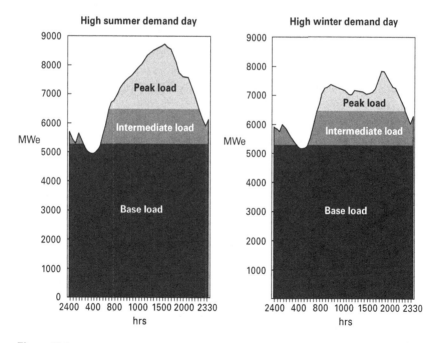

Figure 11.6
Typical load demand curves for electricity in summer vs. winter.

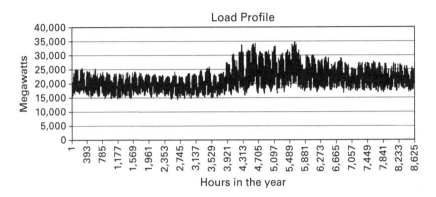

Figure 11.7
An example load demand profile over 1 year by hour.
Source: U.S. Department of Energy.

But when morning comes, power demand surges as people wake up, turn on lights, computers, and other appliances, and begin their workday. Hence, unlike oil demand, for example, which is measured in barrels consumed over a month or a year, electricity demand must be measured hour by hour or even second by second. Furthermore, during a hot summer day, as households and businesses turn on air conditioners to cool homes and offices, peak demand during daylight hours is higher than peak demand on a typical winter day. These fluctuations create a highly volatile electricity load profile over a typical year (figure 11.7).

The load demand profile can be summarized into what is called a "load duration" curve. The load duration curve measures the amount of cumulative hours or duration over the year each particular level of power generation is needed to satisfy demand (figure 11.8).

Because of limitations in the ability to cheaply store power in batteries and the electric grid, supply must match demand in real time (more or less). Hence suppliers must consider not just the absolute level of power capacity needed but how frequently that level of capacity is actually utilized.

This creates a natural division of labor among power suppliers: "baseload" suppliers provide power almost continuously and year-around, while "intermediate" and "peaking" suppliers provide generation capacity used only during the infrequent periods of peak levels for power demand.

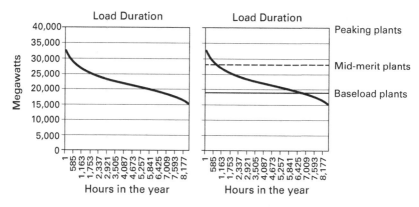

Figure 11.8
An example load duration curve by hour.
Source: U.S. Department of Energy.

As it can be expensive both to build power generation capacity and to activate or deactivate it as power load fluctuates, power suppliers naturally segment themselves into baseload versus peaking power providers. Power suppliers that face low operating costs but high costs to activate and deactivate, such as coal, hydropower, or nuclear power plants, are typically baseload generators, whereas power suppliers that face higher operating costs but can flexibly turn on or off, such as oil- or natural gas–fired power plants, find their comparative advantage as peaking power providers. (I recall here our earlier discussion on the real optionality value to having this flexibility to adjust to economic conditions despite the seemingly higher operating costs relative to baseload power generators).

Solar and wind power generators confront a further challenge. With almost zero operating costs, solar and wind power plants seem to be excellently suited for baseload generation. But rather than intermittency from demand, it is the *supply* of power from these sources that is intermittent, subject to the vagaries of sunlight and wind strength. Hence, even as baseload generators, their unavoidable fluctuations in supply must somehow be accommodated by the rest of the electricity grid.

This differential in relative operating costs leads to the *power dispatch* curve, which is somewhat akin to the familiar supply curve relating prices to the quantity supplied. In this case, the power dispatch curve compares the cumulative power generation *capacity* with the price/cost

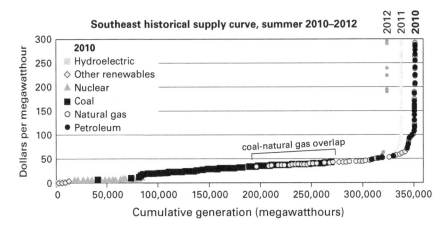

Figure 11.9
A typical power dispatch curve: Southeast historical supply curve, summer 2010–2012.
Source: U.S. Energy Information Administration.

faced by the marginal supplier providing that amount of cumulative supply. Figure 11.9 shows a typical power dispatch curve in the United States in 2010. As shown in the figure, hydroelectric, nuclear, renewable, and coal-fired power plants provided much of the cumulative generation capacity at lower prices on the left-hand side of the curve. But as we move up the capacity scale and approach the domain of intermediate and peaking power plants such as natural gas– and oil-fired plants, the costs suddenly kink upward. And after capacity has been exhausted, prices become effectively infinite as no amount of price can generate power for which there is no capacity, at least not until new capacity is installed. In recent years, lower natural gas prices stemming from the fracking revolution have caused natural gas power plants to eat away at the market share of coal in U.S. baseload power generation.

The price dispatch curve also shows the meritorious pecking order when an ISO calls on a certain amount of power from its generators. Naturally, the cheaper sources of power should be "dispatched" first, before more expensive sources are called on. Only when all cheaper power generation capacity is being fully utilized would the next marginally more expensive source of power generation be activated.

By combing the load duration curve with the price dispatch curve, we can construct the *price duration* curve. Again, a load duration curve relates power demand to the duration of use. A price dispatch curve relates power supply to the cost of dispatch. By matching the two, a

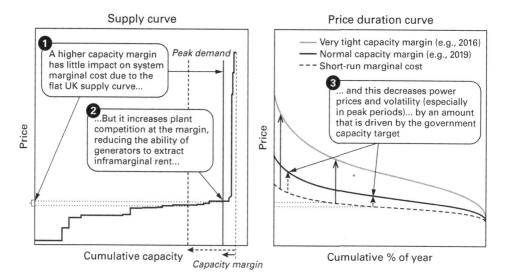

Figure 11.10
An example of a price-duration curve.
Note: Price duration curves are stylized for illustrative purposes.

price duration curve summarizes the time duration of the different equilibrium levels of prices for power (figure 11.10). It is a useful figure to capture the overall economic burden borne by consumers in paying for power and how vulnerable consumers may be to potential price spikes.

Changes in installed capacity, while having usually a limited impact on the marginal price of power at any given time, can nevertheless affect the entire shape of the price duration curve.

Markets for Power Capacity

Our discussion of the price dispatch curve shows how marginal prices kink upward once the power demand in the system approaches the limits of installed capacity. After all, peaking power plants used only very sparingly must charge very high prices when dispatched to make up for sitting idle most of the time. But even the cost of running the most expensive peaking generator is usually lower than the economic damages suffered if an economy does not have access to the power it needs, such as during a brownout or blackout. Development economists point to a lack of reliable power as one of the major headwinds holding back economic growth in many areas of the developing world. In 2003, parts of the northeastern United States suffered a major rolling blackout, with tens of millions of people losing power. The economic cost of the blackout was estimated to range from $4 billion to $10 billion.

The massive economic, social, and political externalities associated with lack of access to power pushes policy makers and regulators to ensure not just that immediate power demand and supply are matched but also that there is sufficient power generation *capacity*. This creates a need for a capacity market, where regulators or system operators pay the private sector to maintain sufficient capacity supply to meet regulatory demand. (Capacity can be measured or rated in precise technical terms as the continuous load-bearing ability of power generation at a predefined point in time.)

There have been various regulatory approaches to ensuring a well-functioning market for power capacity. In the traditional vertically integrated utility model, either the state directly regulates or the state-owned utility chooses the level of capacity sufficient to maximize economic and social welfare. In theory, there is no need for an explicit market as all the economic gains created by installed capacity are captured directly by the state.

Even in deregulated markets, some RTOs and ISOs (such as the New England ISO) may provide an installed capacity requirement (ICR). This sets a fixed amount of capacity mandated to be installed by the ISO's members (figure 11.11).

However, a more sophisticated approach (as, for example, used by PJM or the New York ISO) would introduce an artificial downward-sloping demand curve for capacity set by the regulator, which weighs its desire for more capacity against the price it is willing to pay the private sector to maintain that capacity (figure 11.12). The regulator then sets a target level for capacity, with the price usually set at the calculated cost of new entry (CONE) for a new peaking power plant to be installed.

This regulator's demand curve for capacity would then meet with an offer or supply curve for capacity provided by the private sector (figure 11.13). The actual mechanism to achieve market clearing and equilibrium may be a capacity auction, as generators bid the amounts of rated capacity they would be willing to provide at what price. If the equilibrium amount of capacity is not the desired target, the regulator can shift its demand curve and start the market-clearing process again.

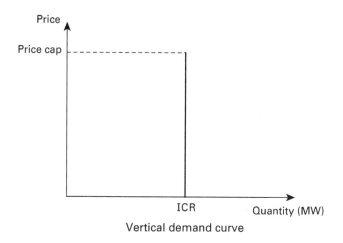

Figure 11.11
Installed capacity requirement.

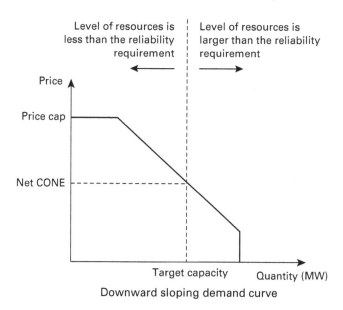

Figure 11.12
A downward-sloping demand curve for capacity.

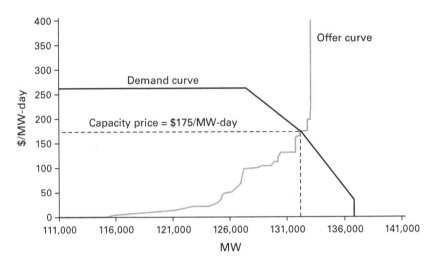

Figure 11.13
Capacity market clearing: ISO/RTO capacity market clearing results.
Source: National Energy Technology Laboratory (NETL).

Some deregulated electricity systems, notably ERCOT in Texas, have no formal mechanism for serving capacity markets, instead relying entirely on the private sector to determine the right level of capacity to install and internalize any externalities through price signals.

Regulators also vary in their approach to determining what target level of capacity is sufficient to meet reliability standards. But it is typically some variation on a forecasted amount of power demand plus some buffer factor.

On top of spot markets for power generation and capacity, some electricity systems also offer forward contracts for power and capacity. Similar in principle to the forward/futures contracts seen for other commodities, forward contracts for power see buyers and sellers commit to trading electricity at a predetermined price at a predefined point in the future (the same applies to capacity contracts). But as electricity cannot be ascribed to a specific supplier, the counterparties must submit to the ISO a balanced scheduled of dispatch that shows the identical amount of electricity that will be supplied by the supplier and consumed by the consumer for each hour. Table 11.2 shows the various presences of forward markets for capacity in various ISOs and RTOs.

Table 11.2
Variation in Capacity Forward Market Provision

ISO/RTO	Capacity market	
	Forward (years)	Forward (months)
California ISO	No	No
ERCOT	No	No
Midwest ISO (voluntary)	No	Yes
ISO New England	Yes	No
New York ISO	No	Yes
PJM	Yes	No
Southwest Power Pool	No	No

Congestion Markets

On top of constraints in power generation capacity, there may also be bottlenecks in transmission capacity to send power from generating sources to consuming sinks. If the flow of electricity exceeds the amount of transmission capacity, then congestion can prevent the free flow of power from the lowest-cost provider. Figure 11.14 shows a simple stylized example of two electricity markets linked by a transmission line. In area A, on the left, a large power plant provides 500 MW of power capacity at a marginal price of $25/MWh. There is also a small town consuming 200 MW every hour. In area B, on the right, there is a small power plant providing only 250 MW of power capacity at a higher marginal price of $35/MWh. But there is a large city demanding 275 MWh.

In the top diagram, the capacity of the transmission line is 500 MW, more than sufficient for power plant A to send 275 MW worth of power to fully meet large city B's demand as well as small town A's. City B would pay the marginal price of $25 to power plant A and the more expensive generation capacity in area 2 would remain underutilized (probably as a peaking plant).

But in the bottom diagram, the transmission capacity is only 250 MW. This is insufficient for power plant A to meet all of city B's demand. Hence, local prices in area B must rise to $35 to incentivize power plant B to supply the remaining 25 MWh.

But if large city B paid only the marginal price of $25 to power plant A, there would be no incentive for power plant A to send the power to B and no economic motive to construct a transmission line to connect

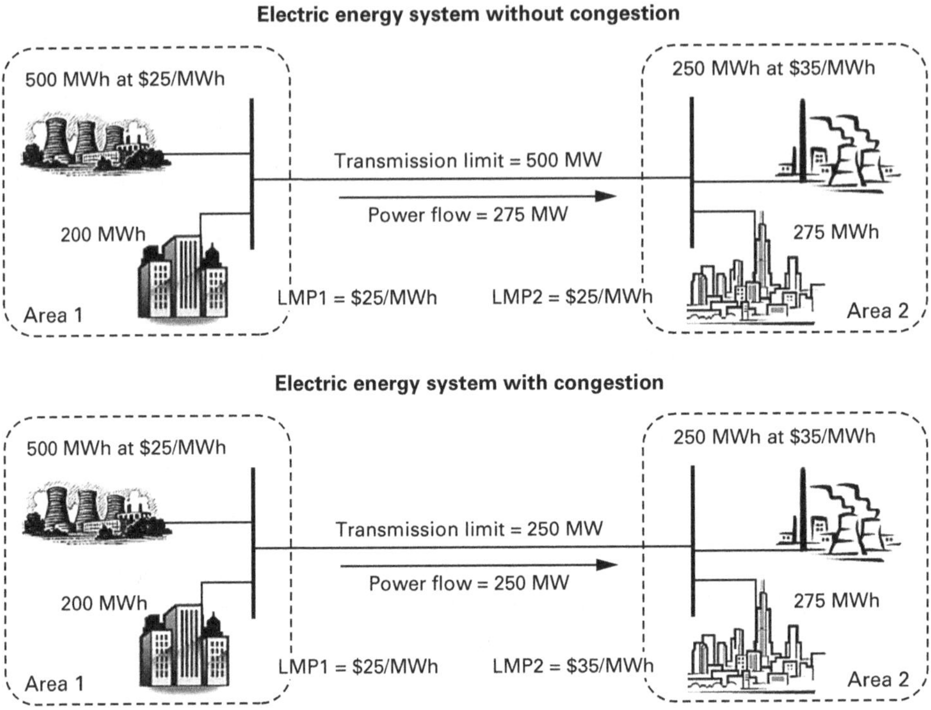

Electric energy system without congestion

500 MWh at $25/MWh

250 MWh at $35/MWh

Transmission limit = 500 MW

Power flow = 275 MW

200 MWh

275 MWh

LMP1 = $25/MWh   LMP2 = $25/MWh

Area 1

Area 2

Electric energy system with congestion

500 MWh at $25/MWh

250 MWh at $35/MWh

Transmission limit = 250 MW

Power flow = 250 MW

200 MWh

275 MWh

LMP1 = $25/MWh   LMP2 = $35/MWh

Area 1

Area 2

Figure 11.14
Simple example of power congestion.
Source: National Energy Technology Laboratory (NETL).

area A with area B. Hence, large city B must face a *locational marginal price* (LMP) of $35 compared to the LMP of only $25 in area A. The $10 spread between A's and B's LMP must go to the holders/operators of the transmission line as a congestion fee, to incentivize them to maintain or even expand transmission capacity.

In practice, RTOs and ISOs collect the margin of LMPs over the underlying marginal cost of generating the power itself. The proceeds are then distributed to the holders of transmission congestion contracts (TCCs), sometimes also known as financial transmission rights (FTRs) or congestion revenue rights (CRRs).

Smart Grids and the Future of Electricity Markets

We conclude this section on electricity markets with a brief discussion of "smart grids" and some thoughts on their promising future. Many existing electricity generation and delivery systems in advanced economies look little changed from half a century ago.

But policy makers, economists, and the private sector all agree that many electricity grids are in need of an overhaul, and the application of new technologies and system processes shows great promise in improving operational efficiencies and reliability. The collective vision for a modernized electricity grid is often loosely grouped into the umbrella term "smart grid."

There is no precise definition, but a "smart grid" typically comprises at least some of the following:

• The increased use of digital information and controls technologies (such as real-time metering, intra-grid communications on status, and automatic distribution) to allow the dynamic optimization of grid operations.
• The deployment and integration of more locally distributed generation capacity, such as rooftop solar panels.
• The provision to consumers of timely information and control options so that demand is more responsive to price and other signals.
• The effective integration of "smart" appliances and other consumer devices in the Internet of Things to the electricity grid.
• Deployment and integration of advanced electricity storage and peak-shaving technologies, including plug-in electric vehicles, and thermal storage air conditioning.

To be sure, certain recent technological developments have sharpened attention on the need for reforming the electricity grid. For example, the recent dramatic declines in the cost of solar (figure 11.15) and wind power have introduced new sources of power with very low operating costs but intermittency caused by fluctuations in sunlight and wind strength.

Distributed power generation from rooftop solar panels means the power generated now sits much more closely to the ultimate consumer, rather than having to be transmitted from a distant power plant. Better batteries and other power storage technologies suggest that power supply and generation may no longer need to perfectly match in real time. The increasing penetration of electric vehicles plugged into the grid may become an unprecedented source of power demand while charging at night but providing surplus power to the grid during the day. Smart meters linked to smart phones may allow retail consumers to respond more elastically to price signals rather than myopically pay

Reported utility-scale solar photovoltaic capital costs (2010–2017)
dollars per watt (2017W_{AC}$)

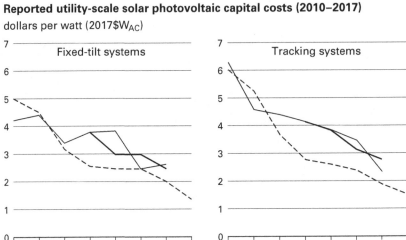

—— U.S. Energy   —— Lawrence Berkeley   – – – National Renewable
Information   National Laboratory   Energy Laboratory
Administration

Figure 11.15
Solar PV costs.
Source: U.S. Energy Information Administration.

an incomprehensible utility bill every month. More communicators and receivers built into various nodes of the grid may help system operators identify and adjust to potential outages and disruptions more effectively. But the penetration of communications technology into the grid is also likely to raise concerns around cybersecurity.

To their cheerleaders, smart grids have the potential to generate large economic gains stemming from lower costs, improved reliability, and superior operational efficiency. But electricity markets are among the most heavily regulated and balkanized markets in the economy, and reducing the barriers to allow for the full and effective deployments of these new technologies and systems may be a heavy challenge for policy makers. But all agree that as these technologies proliferate, the traditional model of electricity generation and delivery will be existentially tested.

Index

Note: Page references followed by *b, f,* and *t* indicate boxes, figures, and tables, respectively. References followed by n indicate notes.